101 "Answers" for New Teachers & Their Mentors

Effective Teaching Tips for Daily Classroom Use

2nd Edition

Annette L. Breaux

Illustrated by L. Susan Brandt

Routledge
Taylor & Francis Group
New York London

First published 2011 by Eye On Education

Published 2013 by Routledge
711 Third Avenue, New York, NY 10017, USA
2 Park Square, Milton Park, Abingdon, Oxon OX14 4RN

Routledge is an imprint of the Taylor & Francis Group, an informa business

Copyright © 2011 Taylor & Francis

Library of Congress Cataloging-in-Publication Data

Breaux, Annette L.
  101 "answers" for new teachers and their mentors : effective teaching tips for daily classroom use / Annette L. Breaux ; illustrations by L. Susan Brandt. -- 2nd ed.
      p. cm.
  ISBN 978-1-59667-182-9
  1. First year teachers—In-service training—Handbooks, manuals, etc. 2. Mentoring in education—Handbooks, manuals, etc. 3. Effective teaching—Handbooks, manuals, etc. I. Title. II. Title: One hundred one "answers" for new teachers and their mentors. III. Title: One hundred and one "answers" for new teachers and their mentors.
  LB2844.1.N4B74 2011
  371.102--dc22

                                                        2011006794

Cover Designer: Dave Strauss

ISBN: 978-1-596-67182-9 (pbk)

Also Available from Eye On Education

REAL Teachers, REAL Challenges, REAL Solutions:
25 Ways to Handle the Challenges of the Classroom Effectively
Annette L. Breaux & Elizabeth Breaux

50 Ways to Improve Student Behavior:
Simple Solutions to Complex Challenges
Annette L. Breaux & Todd Whitaker

Seven Simple Secrets:
What the BEST Teachers Know and Do!
Annette L. Breaux & Todd Whitaker

10 Days to Maximum Teaching Success
Annette L. Breaux

101 Poems for Teachers
Annette L. Breaux

How the Best Teachers Differentiate Instruction
Elizabeth Breaux & Monique Boutte Magee

How The Best Teachers Avoid The 20 Most Common Teaching Mistakes
Elizabeth Breaux

How to Reach and Teach ALL Students—Simplified
Elizabeth Breaux

Classroom Management—Simplified
Elizabeth Breaux

The Passion-Driven Classroom:
A Framework for Teaching and Learning
Angela Maiers & Amy Sandvold

Helping Students Motivate Themselves:
Practical Answers to Classroom Challenges
Larry Ferlazzo

What Do You Say When...?
Best Practice Language for Improving Student Behavior
Hal Holloman & Peggy H. Yates

*I dedicate this book to the memory of my grandfather, Pop,
the greatest teacher I have ever known.*

About the Author

Annette Breaux is one of the most entertaining and informative authors and speakers in education today. She leaves her audiences with practical techniques to implement in their classrooms immediately. Administrators agree that they see results from teachers the next day.

A former classroom teacher, curriculum coordinator, and teacher induction coordinator, she is also the author of Louisiana FIRST, a statewide induction program for new teachers. Annette has coauthored a book with Dr. Harry Wong on new teacher induction.

Her other writings include: *REAL Teachers, REAL Challenges, REAL Solutions; Seven Simple Secrets: What the BEST Teachers Know and Do; 50 Ways to Improve Student Behavior: Simple Solutions to Complex Challenges,* and *101 Poems for Teachers.*

Teachers who have read Annette's writings or heard Annette speak agree that they come away with user-friendly information, heartfelt inspiration, and a much-needed reminder that theirs is the most noble of all professions—teaching.

About the Illustrator

L. Susan Brandt is a freelance illustrator who lives in Dallas, Texas. Her mediums include pencil, pen-and-ink, pastels, and watercolors. She also illustrated Breaux's *101 Poems for Teachers.*

Contents

Instruction 41

Professionalism: Attitudes and Behaviors of Effective Teachers 65

Motivation and Rapport **97**

A Teacher's Influence 127

Plus 7 More! 137

Conclusion 147

Foreword

This book is THE book I wish I had had when I first started teaching. Consider the following:

- **New teachers need support,** from day one, if they are going to succeed in their classrooms.
- Though many new teachers DO receive **induction support** provided by their schools or districts, still many do not. Regardless, new teachers can use as much support as we can provide.
- **Many mentors receive one-shot training and nothing more**. The more training a mentor receives, the better he/she is able to mentor. However, a mentor is only ONE person, usually with his/her own classroom. A mentor alone cannot be responsible for the success of a new teacher.
- We, as educators, tend to **"assume" too much regarding what new teachers are ready to handle** in the classroom.
- **New teachers want answers**, yet they are often afraid to ask for help for fear of appearing incompetent.
- There are some **simple and basic teaching strategies that can help any teacher to be more effective.** New teachers deserve access to all of these from day one!

Above are my reasons for writing this book. There is no rocket science here, just simple answers to complex challenges along with tips that will help new teachers to be better teachers, mentors to be better teachers, and mentors to be better mentors. If you are neither a new teacher nor a mentor, read on anyway. You'll find that the strategies in this book will be beneficial to any teacher at the elementary, middle, or secondary level seeking to be more effective.

I share this book with you along with my love of children, my love of teaching, my belief that teachers touch lives, and my absolute conviction that every child is someone special. Every child deserves a capable, competent, caring teacher. The children are our future, and as teachers, we help to mold that future every single day.

Introduction

To the Teacher

Do you love children? Do you want to make a difference? Do you want to have a positive impact on young lives? Of course you do! In order to accomplish that, you have chosen the most noble of all professions—teaching. Teaching is a highly skilled craft, requiring patience, commitment, dedication, sincere love of children, charisma, confidence, and competence. **As a teacher, you will affect the lives of each of your students on a daily basis.**

If you are a new teacher, you know that it is your sincere desire to be successful, to inspire, to touch lives, and to make a difference. Yet many of you, through no fault of your own, lack the necessary training to be effective from your very first day of teaching. Hopefully, you have signed on with a school district that provides induction training. Induction is a highly structured, systematic means of training and supporting new teachers, beginning before their first day of teaching and continuing throughout their first two or three years. Mentoring is one vital component of the induction process. **If you have not been assigned a mentor, find one.** There are many capable, competent, caring teachers out there who are more than willing to share their expertise with novices. **You cannot and will not be expected to know everything from day one.** You'll need guidance. And although mentors cannot provide for all of the needs of new teachers, they can be valuable assets to new teachers. So seek out the most positive, enthusiastic, successful teacher on the faculty and enlist his/her support to help ensure your success in the classroom.

Remember, you are helping to mold the future, and your influence will long outlive you. You are a teacher. What an honor, and what a tremendous responsibility! Rise to the challenge!

To the Mentor

If you have been selected to serve as a mentor for a new teacher, you should be honored. Someone, somewhere, has recognized your successes in the classroom and your leadership qualities. And, hopefully, you have been well trained in the art of mentoring. If not, please insist on it! **No matter how good your teaching skills may be, mentoring is different from teaching, and it requires structured training.**

As a mentor, you will play the role of teacher, friend, guide, coach, and role model. You will be expected to provide support, encouragement, a listening ear, a welcoming shoulder, constructive feedback, and suggestions for improvement.

You will be required to exhibit professionalism, the ability to plan and organize, a love of children and teaching, excellence in teaching, effective communication skills, coaching skills, conferencing skills, and an optimistic attitude. You will be responsible for maintaining confidentiality; sharing knowledge, skills, and information with the new teacher; meeting frequently with the new teacher; observing the new teacher; providing demonstration lessons for the new teacher; familiarizing the new teacher with school policies, procedures, and culture; and participating in ongoing professional improvement activities. And above all, you must be understanding, supportive, trustworthy, empathetic, innovative, knowledgeable, open-minded, reform-minded, and committed.

Does this sound a little overwhelming? Well, rest assured that your efforts will be rewarded a hundred-fold, as **you will be positively affecting the lives of the new teachers you mentor. This will have a direct impact on every student that will ever enter the new teachers' classroom doors.**

Congratulations on being selected to mentor a new teacher, and thank you for accepting the challenge.

Common New Teacher Challenges

Though all new teachers face a variety of challenges in the classroom, there are several that seem common to most. In fact, these are the same challenges that remain common for many veteran teachers throughout their careers. These challenges include dealing with the overall management of the classroom; effectively handling discipline problems; dealing with difficult students, coworkers, and parents; planning effectively; managing time wisely; remaining calm and professional in the face of unnerving situations; utilizing the most effective teaching strategies; accommodating individual differences in students; engaging students in critical thinking; etc.

This book is specifically designed to assist teachers in dealing with such challenges effectively. It is not loaded with fads, trends, educational jargon of the day, or the latest of educational innovations. Rather, it provides tried and true suggestions and techniques that will work for anyone willing to implement them. Quite simply, this book will truly help to enhance both teaching and learning at any grade level. The opportunity to be the most effective teacher you can be awaits you, and the fact that you are reading this book says that you are seizing the opportunity and welcoming the challenge.

How to Use This Book

This book can be used in one of several ways. It is designed primarily to facilitate discussion between the mentor and the new teacher and to **provide ideas and promote effective teaching for both mentors and new teachers.** Of course, the ideas and teaching tips are universal and thus can be used by any teacher seeking to be more effective. All of the suggestions are easy to implement and will prove beneficial to both teachers and students. The 101 tips are divided into the following subheadings: *Classroom Management, Planning, Instruction, Professionalism: Attitudes and Behaviors of Effective Teachers, Motivation and Rapport,* and *A Teacher's Influence.* Therefore, if a new teacher is working on establishing effective classroom management, he/she should use the suggestions found under that section. If a mentor needs to "brush up" on management skills so as to serve as a role model for the new teacher, the tips found there will be more than beneficial. Feel free to pick and choose any and all that seem appropriate for your classroom. However, use all of them if you want to truly enhance your effectiveness whether you are a mentor, a first-time teacher, or any teacher seeking to better your skills.

Again, **the very fact that you are reading this says that you are a dedicated teacher who chooses to make a difference in the lives of the students you teach.** This book will help to pave the way.

Classroom Management

How Does One Manage a Classroom?

"How does one manage a classroom? Is it really rocket science?
For I've been told it's difficult to control so much student defiance."
Well, management is about the teacher, and what the teacher expects
Because everything about the teacher absolutely affects
How students will or won't respond, how they will or will not act,
And with excellent classroom management, students behave well. That's a fact!
So set clear rules and procedures, and show how you want things done
And remember that on the scale of importance, consistency is number one!
Consistency in how you treat each one, consistency in your preparation,
Consistency in being professional, regardless of your level of frustration,
Consistency in saying what you mean and meaning what you say,
Consistency in making every student feel special every day,
Consistency in your refusal to give up on anyone,
Consistency in helping students to see a task through 'til it's done,
Consistency in good attitude, for your attitude sets the tone,
Consistency in being available, so that no student feels alone,
Consistency in helping every child to know he can succeed,
Yes, consistency is the key to classroom management, indeed!
And consistency is not difficult—just be consistent at being consistent—
And soon your discipline problems will be a memory that is distant!

A.L.B.

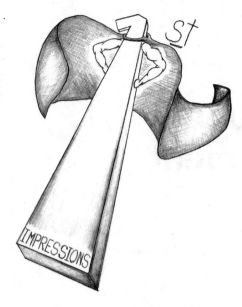

Since you never get a second chance to make a first impression, please take care that what you wear is a positive expression!

Off to a Positive Start

First impressions are vital! **In the classroom, your first impression can set the tone for the entire school year.** Often, teachers make the mistake of diving into "teaching the content" from the very first day of school. Instead, it is critically important that you take the time to let the students know who you are, that you allow them the opportunity to begin to tell you who they are, and that you immediately set them up for success. One way to do this is through structure. If you are going through new teacher induction training, then you already know how your first day of school should be structured. If not, find out from your mentor teacher or other successful veteran teachers exactly what they do on the first day of school. **FACT: The most successful teachers begin with structured procedures from the beginning.** (See Tips 2 and 3 for more on procedures.)

Here are a few MUSTS for **beginning the school year on a positive note**:

- ♦ Greet your students at the door with a huge smile on your face.
- ♦ Be organized and prepared. Plan every minute of your first day beforehand.
- ♦ Have some type of appealing assignment (possibly an interest inventory) awaiting students so that they can get busy immediately upon entering the classroom.
- ♦ Remain calm, pleasant, and positive. If you're smiling, they won't know you're nervous!
- ♦ Share your expectations and tell them what they can expect from you and your class.
- ♦ Tell them you are so excited to be their teacher, and thank them for being in your class.
- ♦ Express your belief that they will ALL be successful!

If you want to get off to a positive start, don't just teach content, but reach the heart.
Convince your students, first, that you care; then your teaching can take them anywhere!

Without procedures and routines, chaos intervenes. But when routines and procedures are established and expected, with learning and laughter your students will be infected!

The Importance of Classroom Management

Contrary to popular belief, **discipline is NOT the number one problem in the classroom.** Rather, **the lack of clear, structured, well-rehearsed procedures and routines is what causes most discipline problems.** So what do the most successful teachers do? From the first day, they establish clear routines and procedures, and students are shown and told exactly what is expected of them. These teachers are also aware of the definition of classroom management: **Classroom management involves everything you do to make your classroom run smoothly**: How you arrange the furniture to facilitate learning, how you expect students to enter and exit your classroom, where you stand when you are teaching to ensure that you are in proximity to all of your students, how quickly you pace activities, how you establish expectations for student behavior and so on. In other words, a good teacher plans EVERYTHING.

If you want what all teachers want—to experience little or no discipline problems with your students—then it is important that you have a clear, concise classroom management plan. But please do not reinvent the wheel. Implement the basic tried and true management techniques of the most successful teachers that you will continue to read about throughout this book. Aside from reading this book, you may want to read the well-known, practical, common sense approach to classroom management: *The First Days of School* by Harry and Rosemary Wong.

FACT: Just as a bus cannot transport students to school without tires, even if the bus is in perfect mechanical condition, a teacher cannot teach ANYTHING to students until classroom management is in place, even if he/she is very knowledgeable about the content. Management is just as important to learning as tires are to getting a bus from point A to point B. **Clearly-established procedures and routines are the most important part of any good classroom management plan.**

When students are shown just what is expected, behavior problems will soon be corrected. Learning and laughter are what you are after, and you can have these. Set procedures, please.

For what kinds of things should procedures be set? For anything that you don't want to regret!

Have Procedures for Almost Everything

Some activities lend themselves to creative expression. Others do not. *Designing* an automobile lends itself to creative expression. *Assembling* the automobile does not. The same is true for classroom management. **In order to successfully manage a classroom of students or any group of people, clearly defined procedures—consistent ways of doing things—must be established.** Take 30 students and do not tell them how you want a task done. They will each make up numerous ways to perform that task. Many of these ways will be unacceptable. You see, 30 students doing things their own way for even one task will allow for endless possibilities of how the task will be accomplished. This is good when teaching them how to think, but not so good when teaching them how to behave. So what kinds of activities require procedures in the classroom? **Any activity that does not lend itself to creative expression requires procedures.** For instance, you would not want your students "creating" ways of entering your classroom, sharpening their pencils, turning in assignments, moving into groups, or walking to the lunchroom. As the person in charge of managing a group of students, it is your responsibility to establish procedures in order to ensure the smooth operation of your classroom environment.

The following are a few examples of activities that require procedures:

- Entering and exiting the classroom
- Passing in papers
- Asking for permission to speak
- Knowing what to do with your book bag when you enter the classroom
- Asking a question
- Working cooperatively in groups
- Knowing what to do if you have finished your work and others have not
- Turning in homework assignments, etc.

Tell your students what you expect, show them how you expect things to be done, practice the procedures with them, and reinforce as necessary. And please remember that the act of practicing procedures is not something for elementary students only. Consider the fact that professional football teams practice the same procedures over and over and over, every day! Oh, and always pretend to assume that the students simply forgot the procedure. If you let them know that you think they are just being defiant by not following the procedure, then they are controlling you and will continue to do so. Instead, calmly say, "Oh I see that a few of you have forgotten the procedure and need a little more practice." No big deal! And even if it IS a big deal to you, don't let them know that. Remain calm and simply practice the procedure with them again.

When from the procedures students stray, practice, practice, practice away!

If the classroom hums like a well-rehearsed choir, then to misbehave I lose my desire...

Discipline

The terms *discipline* and *classroom management* are often mistakenly used synonymously. **Discipline is only one part of classroom management, albeit a vital one.** Your discipline plan (and you must have one) should consist of a set of a few rules. If a student breaks a rule, there is a definite consequence. This consequence is not contingent upon the frustration level of the teacher at the time the rule is broken, but rather is predetermined as the plan is being devised. **Students are told what the classroom rules are and what the consequences are for not following any of the rules.**

Rules are devised to set limits, to help maintain order, and to protect people. On our public highways, there are speed limits. If the limit is exceeded, there is a consequence—a speeding ticket. This consequence is predetermined. Motorists are well aware of the consequence of exceeding the speed limit, just as students should be well aware of the consequences of breaking rules in your classroom. Therefore, devise a discipline plan and enforce it consistently. And please ensure that your rules cover serious offenses only. Teachers often get into trouble, creating discipline problems, when they post ten, fifteen, twenty or so rules for the class, many of which relate to minor offenses. An example would be *talking*, which is procedural in nature. (For a practically foolproof way of getting students to stop talking out of turn, see Teaching Tip 102 in the "Plus 7 More" section.) An example of a serious offense that would require a rule would be something like the act of hitting. Most teachers would agree that this is a serious offense and that there should be a rule and consequence established to regulate this behavior.

Have you ever noticed that the very best teachers have very few discipline problems? The real key to their success does not lie in the way that they discipline their students after the rules have been broken. Rather, they have established ways of preventing most, if not all, behavior problems through the structure of their classroom management plans along with their pleasant demeanors and proactive approaches to dealing with students. The simple fact is that in a well-managed environment there are very few discipline problems. The classroom hums like a well-rehearsed choir!

With good management in place, there's no need to be mean, and discipline problems are few and far between.

The more YOU behave out of care and concern, the more the students behave and the more they learn!

Use the "Are You All Right?" Technique

The "Are You All Right?" technique is based on the simple premise that **children who believe you care about them are much more apt to behave.** It works like this: If a student is doing something inappropriate during class such as picking on others, talking excessively, refusing to do work, etc., simply step out into the hall with him/her and ask, "Are you all right?" with a sincere look of concern—not aggravation—on your face. Usually the student will answer, "Yes," with a look of disbelief. Then say, "Well, I'm asking because the way you were behaving was inappropriate and so unlike you." (Okay, so you're stretching the truth a little, because the way he was acting may have been quite typical...) Then say, "I knew that something must be bothering you for you to be acting that way, so I just wanted to know if you were all right and to let you know that if anything is bothering you, I'm here for you if you need to talk." That's it. You simply walk back into the classroom and resume teaching. And guess what happens! The student almost always abandons the misbehavior. And now you've accomplished several things: You've made the point that the behavior was inappropriate, you've maintained the student's dignity, you've acted out of concern instead of frustration, and you've let the student know that you care about him. What more could you want to accomplish?

Said the student to his teacher: "Once I believe you care about me, I'll behave much better. Try it. You'll see!"

When "I'm happy to see you" is what your face is telling, students are more likely to buy the content you're selling!

Greet Students Daily

If you walk into Walmart, you will be greeted by someone you very likely do not know. This person's job is to welcome every customer who walks into the store. When you walk into a department store, you will be greeted by a sales clerk and told that they will be happy to assist you. When you walk onto an airplane, you are greeted and welcomed. When you go to a restaurant, you are greeted, seated, and waited upon. Why do these businesses spend so much money, time, and effort in assuring that their patrons feel welcomed upon entering their places of business? The reason is that **people appreciate and respond to environments where they are made to feel welcomed and special.** The same holds true for the classroom. All too often, teachers are busy making last minute preparations for class and thus do not stand at the door smiling and welcoming every student as they enter. Not greeting your students every day may be one of the biggest mistakes you could ever make.

I once worked with a negative teacher who, to her credit, wanted to become more positive. I suggested that she stand out in the hallway and greet her students as they walked into the room. I stayed inside of the classroom, and I could not see her, because she was out in the hallway. The students walked in with looks of shock on their faces, but the best part was when one young man stood in front of his classmates and saluted and said, "We're all going down today! She looks way too happy!" Funny as that was, the point is that if you don't typically greet your students, they may be a little shocked and disbelieving upon your first attempt. Stick with it however. Students will believe you're a "changed person" within a few days of greeting them.

Students who are welcomed as they enter the class are much more likely to "buy" what you are "selling." A simple smile and a genuine welcome will set the stage, every day, for a positive experience with your students. Just a handshake and a personal greeting offered to each student every day will help to earn the trust and respect of your students. Students like to be where they feel welcomed, and students succeed in positive environments.

Happy, successful students? Any teacher will say "hello" to that!

The teacher looked for misbehavior in every cranny and nook, and the classroom became a chaotic place that the students overtook...

Learn What to Overlook

Children are not perfect, and neither are we. Teachers who expect perfect behavior from their students are being unrealistic and are inviting disappointment. For example, if you are expecting that your students will never whisper to one another, you've lost touch with reality. And if the occasional "whispering" is not overly distracting, overlook it. It's not a big deal. However, when many students begin talking and are off task, this should not be overlooked. The fact is that children will talk. They will make mistakes. They will act inappropriately at times. Why? Because they are children. Wise teachers know that if they get nitpicky about every little imperfection, they will literally run around putting out fires all day long, leaving little, if any, time for teaching.

The following are a few examples of behaviors that effective teachers tend to overlook: tapping a pencil on the desk, quiet laughter between two students, an occasional whisper from one student to another, a student slouching in his desk, a student getting distracted for a brief period of time, etc.

There is no "cookbook recipe" listing exactly what can and cannot be overlooked in the classroom, but the following should do the trick:

Take a cup of common sense and mix with heaping spoonfuls of patience, understanding, consistency, positive expectations, and an enthusiastic attitude about everything you teach. Pour in a heart full of love and bake for one school year.

Reprove a student confidentially, and behavior will improve exponentially!

Handle Discipline Problems Discreetly

I call it the **Faculty Meeting Rule**, and it goes like this: **Do not say or do anything to your students in your classroom that you would not feel comfortable having your own principal say or do to you in a faculty meeting.** Wow! Imagine if all teachers treated all students the way these same teachers would expect to be treated by their own principals! The Faculty Meeting Rule serves as an excellent gauge, because just as teachers are among their peers in a faculty meeting and would not appreciate being singled out and embarrassed in front of their peers, students are among their peers in the classroom and the same holds true for them. How would you feel if your principal singled you out and reprimanded you publicly for speaking during a faculty meeting? Most teachers would be mortified! Or how would you feel if the principal announced the results of each teacher's observations in the midst of everyone else? These are issues that should be discussed privately.

As teachers, we each have our own private "office." It's located right outside the classroom door, away from the rest of the students. Though it is not always possible to deal with every discipline challenge in total privacy, teachers should always use discretion. Discretion sometimes simply involves talking to a student at his desk in a quiet tone. Public reprimand simply does not work. It actually breeds resentment in students. Students will appreciate being treated with respect and will recognize that you value their privacy and dignity. FACT: A student is much more likely to correct his misbehavior when his dignity has been maintained. Also, notice that a student is not nearly as "tough" when you deal with him one on one, away from his audience, his classmates.

To my teacher: Please use discretion with me rather than aggression with me, and please have a private session with me when you discuss my behavior transgression with me!

Sending students to the office for minor aggravations sends a message that you cannot handle typical teacher frustrations!

Handle Your Own Discipline Problems

It is often said that **90 percent of a school's discipline referrals comes from 10 percent of the teachers.** Can it be that the 10 percent have all of the *problem* students? Not likely. What is more probable is that the remaining 90 percent of the teachers are handling their own discipline problems. They know that students respect teachers who are both capable of and willing to maintain a positive, active, and safe learning environment. They know that students respect teachers who are in control (not "controlling," but rather "in" control). This is not to say that effective teachers never have to refer student discipline problems to the office, but these incidences are rare and are thus taken seriously by both the administrator and the students. **Common misbehaviors such as talking, inattentiveness, attention seeking, teasing, etc. should be handled by the teacher.**

When a teacher sends a student to the office for a minor offense such as not turning in homework or failing to pay attention, the teacher is admitting to that student, to the rest of the students, and to the administration that he/she is not capable of handling typical classroom challenges. From here forward, the students know that they possess the power to control the teacher! This is the last thing you ever want your students thinking. Therefore, do what the most effective teachers do and, with only rare exceptions, handle your own discipline problems.

Don't rely on administration to handle every trial and tribulation, but rather be in control of your own domain and the students' respect you will certainly gain!

A Little Praise

*I helped a girl at school one day who had fallen and scraped
her knee*
I only did what any kid would've done if he were me
Then the teacher said that I was one of the nicest kids she'd met
*And I thought to myself, "Well that's because she doesn't know
me yet."*
*'Cause I'm really not so nice sometimes—I say and do bad
things*
*I don't always finish my homework or come in right when
the bell rings*
But my teacher keeps on thinking that I'm really extra nice
So whenever I'm around her, I'm nice, not once, but twice
I even work much harder when I am in her class
Instead of going really slow, I finish extra fast
She always takes the time to notice everything good I do
*She's told me I'm special so many times that I think it's
becoming true.*

A.L.B.

Catch Students Behaving

Think back to your teacher training days and try to recall the class entitled "How to Catch Students Behaving." Do you remember that class? No? Think about this: As teachers, **we are trained to recognize problems, diagnose the causes of the problems, and then respond accordingly to solve these problems.** That's a fact, and it is a necessary skill that any good teacher must possess. But how many of us were ever trained to recognize good behavior, diagnose what's causing the good behavior, and then foster that behavior so that it will continue? Not many. As teachers, we all have "eyes in the backs of our heads" and can spot a child misbehaving from a mile away! Again, this is a good skill to possess. But an even more important skill is to be able to **use those same "eyes in the backs of our heads" to spot a child behaving well and encourage that good behavior or kind deed.** A simple "Thanks for raising your hand" or "I really appreciate the cooperation I'm observing with this group" can work wonders. Students crave our attention, and they will usually do whatever it takes to get it. When they learn that they are much more apt to get your attention by behaving, they begin behaving. Teachers who focus more on *good* behavior than on *mis*behavior experience fewer discipline problems. So be on the lookout for good behavior. You'll begin to notice it everywhere!

If you look for what's right, then maybe you might
See things that are good and less of what's bad
And more of what's happy and less of what's sad
And when students know that you are the kind
Who goes out of your way to search for and find
The best inside of everyone
Then most behavior problems are over and done!

There's no bloom without a bud
Without dirt, there is no mud
Without a fall, there is no thud
Without a cut, there is no blood
So nip a problem in the bud
And prevent the mud, blood, and thud!

Be Proactive

Do you know what it looks like when students begin to get bored? When a child is upset? When a student is "thinking" about misbehaving? Anyone who has ever been around children or who has ever *been* a child can easily answer yes to all of these questions. And anyone who can answer yes to these questions can be proactive. **Being "proactive" simply means recognizing *potential* problems and stopping them before they become *actual* problems.** Here is an example that epitomizes a teacher using a proactive approach to problem solving—or rather, problem preventing. I went to the door of a classroom one day to speak with a teacher. As we were speaking, she noticed that Tremain was out of his desk, heading toward Jonathon to hit him. The teacher immediately looked at him and said, "Tremain, thank you so much for going over to help Jonathon. I was just bragging to Ms. Breaux about how helpful you all are in this class, and there you are demonstrating it. Thank you, Tremain. I really appreciate your thoughtfulness." Tremain, totally caught off guard and completely distracted from his original *mission*, walked on over to Jonathon and helped him with his work. This, of course, was how the teacher handled every potential problem. She recognized it and immediately *broke the pattern of the student*. She turned the potentially negative situation around and always managed to make it a positive one. If students were appearing bored, she changed the activity. When a child walked into class looking upset, she spoke to the child privately, listened, and expressed concern. When a child was contemplating an inappropriate behavior, she often asked the child a question, completely unrelated to what was about to happen, in order to defuse the potential problem. It worked for this teacher, and it will work for you. Oh, and speaking of working, children work much harder and behave much better in the classrooms of proactive teachers.

Recognize what I'm about to do
And redirect my attention to you
And use clever ways to help me to
Never know that you knew what I was about to do!

Have you ever noticed how much pent up energy students have as they burst out of the schoolhouse doors at the end of the day?

Provide Frequent Stretch Breaks

Have you ever had to sit in a meeting for over an hour, or, better yet, an entire day? Have you gotten restless and/or bored? Have you noticed the talking that goes on between teachers during such meetings? Why is this? Basically, it's because teachers are active people. They are accustomed to moving around, *doing* things, and rarely sitting still during the day. The teachers walk out of the school building at the end of the day looking exhausted because they've been working all day long. So why is it that the students look so energetic? Could it be that they've been literally sitting most of the day? **FACT: Students are often off task or talk at inappropriate times because they are restless and in desperate need of some action.** What we need to see is the students looking exhausted at the end of the school day. Here is a simple, two-part way to make sure that that happens:

1. **Become aware of the amount of time that your students are expected to remain seated during your classes.** Students need to be kept so busy that they don't have time to misbehave or be off task. This is not to say that the desks should be removed from the classrooms. Many classroom activities require students to be seated in their desks. But teachers who are *aware* of the energy just waiting to come out of those young bodies and minds use that awareness to their advantage.

2. **When you notice that students have been seated for more than thirty minutes or so (or even less for younger students), provide a stretch break.**

   I recently observed a teacher who, out of nowhere, it appeared, would say to the class, "Okay, when I say 'go,' you will have forty-five seconds to stand up, stretch, and talk to your neighbors. Remember, however, that when I say 'stop,' you must be seated and quiet immediately." During a one-hour lesson, he did this three times. The students followed the procedure beautifully, and it appeared that they were accustomed to doing this. I also noted that the teaching activities moved quickly, the pace was steady, and the students remained on task throughout the lesson. Following the lesson, I asked the teacher about the frequent breaks. He smiled and said, "Oh, that. I don't know about you, but I know that I can't manage to sit still for more than twenty minutes at a time, and I'm much older than my students, so I don't have near the energy that they do. I make it a practice to provide frequent stretch breaks. As you probably noticed, the breaks don't last long, but they work! I've also noticed that students are able to maintain more of a focus if they are allowed to stand up, stretch, talk a little, and keep their blood flowing. It literally re-energizes them, and I need for my students to focus all the energy they have on what we're learning."

He went on to explain that even during times of active student participation involving group work, he still took time to give the students stretch breaks so that they could re-energize and refocus. "My students work hard in here," he said. "I want them to leave my classroom enlightened, inspired, and a little exhausted every day. If they don't, then I'm not doing my job."

Give them a stretch break to get their blood flowing
And they'll better display what they're learning and knowing
And you'll see the growth from the seeds you are sowing
And they'll reap the rewards from the knowledge you're bestowing!

The farther you stand from a student, the less likely he is to be prudent.

Use Proximity

If I were to ask your students, "Where does your teacher usually stand?" could they answer that question? Would they possibly point to a very distinct area, usually in the front of the classroom? If your answer is yes, read on.

A teacher once asked me, "Have you ever noticed that the 'problem' students always gravitate toward the back of the classroom? It never fails," he said. "My behavior problems, every year, come from the back of the room." Upon observing this teacher, I noted that he never ventured past the front row of desks in the classroom. The farther back the students sat, the more they talked! Seated in the back of the room myself, I was almost tempted to join in the conversation, as I felt completely removed from both the teacher and the lesson. All the action was in the front of the room, so the students in the back created their own action. I also noted that the only time the students in the back were acknowledged was with verbal reprimands or the *teacher eye* when the noise escalated. After the lesson, I asked the teacher if he would be willing to attempt an experiment in order to possibly alleviate the problems with his "problem" students. He agreed to participate. The experiment involved his use of proximity. For one week, I asked him to spend his teaching time moving around the classroom, spending time among all of the students. He also agreed that when a student was talking or was off task, he would calmly move closer to that student without the use of the *teacher eye* or verbal reprimands. One week later, I sat in the same classroom, but it definitely did not *feel* like the same classroom. Amazingly, the "problem" students were now actively involved in the lessons. Instead of talking to one another, they were involved in discussions with the teacher. And, not to my surprise, the teacher was noticeably more enthusiastic in his delivery. "I can't believe it," he said to me after the lesson. "How could I have missed that? I've been blaming the students during the five years I've been teaching. And the answer was so simple. I'm actually enjoying teaching now, and I can tell that the students are enjoying my lessons more." The simple fact is that physical distance equals mental distance in the classroom. So get in there with your students.

The farther your distance, the more their resistance
So teach in your classroom like coaches in a huddle do
And make it less likely that their actions will befuddle you.

Be Prepared for the Answer

If you're going to ask a question, be prepared
*   for the answer*
Or consider yourself a wooden floor where
*   each student becomes a dancer.*
They'll dance all over your question;
*   they'll outsmart you every time*
And you will end up treating them
*   as if they've committed a crime.*
So be careful about your questions;
*   only ask what you want to know*
And chances are better you'll be less
*   of a fretter,*
And your temper you won't have to
*   blow!*

A.L.B.

Do Not Provoke Defensiveness

The following are actual teacher questions and the resulting student answers:

Teacher: How many times do I have to tell you?
Student: 6,284.

Teacher: Don't you have any home training?
Student: My dad is in jail, and my mom is on drugs!

Teacher: Do you want me to send you to the office?
Student: Actually, yes. It would be a pleasant diversion.

Teacher: Do you have a problem?
Student: No, but you look like you could use some anger-management training!

Teacher: Don't you know this material?
Student: If I did, then I guess you'd be out of a job!

In all of the above scenarios, can you guess what the teachers' reactions were? The teachers were horrified and highly insulted. Though I am not, in any way, suggesting that the students' answers were the most appropriate ones, I am suggesting that these teachers *set themselves up* for the answers they received. These teachers were acting out of anger and frustration. In actuality, they were fueling the exact behaviors they were trying to diminish. The simple fact is that sarcastic questions provoke sarcastic answers. And, as we will discuss in Tip 85, there is no place for sarcasm in the classroom. If a student is struggling, instead of asking, "Do you have a problem?" in a sarcastic tone, simply say, "I notice that you're struggling with this, and I'd like to help." Then do just that—assist the student. In the last question and answer above, the student actually made a very valid point: If students knew all the answers and exhibited perfect behavior and ample amounts of self-motivation, we would all be out of a job!

Give a student nothing to do,
And he'll find something to do, it's true.
But note that what he finds to do
Is no task you would ever want him
to pursue!

Avoid "Down" Time

"Down" time consists of any time that a student has nothing to do. When does "down" time typically occur in the classroom? It usually occurs when students finish an assignment early, when the teacher finishes a lesson before the end of the class period, or during transitions from one subject to the next. That was the problem, and here is the solution: Simply put, **the way to avoid "down" time is to structure every minute of the entire class period.** In other words, when giving an assignment, provide structured activities for early finishers. A note of caution here: Just because a student finishes early does not mean that he has completed the assignment correctly. Determine that first, and then you will know whether to provide enrichment activities or remediation activities at that point. Regardless, the student will keep busy. Next, do not make the mistake of under-planning where you may be left with several empty minutes at the end of the class period. When students have nothing to do, they'll find something to do, and it usually won't be to your liking! Therefore, **teach from "bell to bell."**

Regarding transitions, implement structured procedures that make the transitions smooth and efficient. My favorite example comes from my own classroom experiences. I noted that during transitions, where I would instruct the students to put one set of materials away and prepare for the next subject, it was inevitable that the following would occur: Some students would be ready to go in seconds, some were seated on the floor looking inside of their desks, some would start cleaning the insides of their desks, some would engage in conversations with others, etc. And these transitions were eating away at valuable teaching and learning time. So I began to do the following, which has continued to work wonders for me and for many others with whom I have shared the technique—at all age levels, I might add. I discovered that students enjoy being "timed" during transitions, and I used that discovery to implement a procedure. I would say, "Okay, don't move until I say 'go.' But when I say 'go,' I want for you to pick up your reading books and get out your language projects from yesterday. I'm going to be timing you, and the world record for seventh graders is 9.243 seconds. (Of course, I was just fabricating this!)

When you're ready to go, give me a 'thumbs up.' And when all thumbs are up, I'll record your time. Go!" Amazingly, it worked! Within seconds, all students were ready to go and anxious to see if they had set the new world record. Even more amazingly, I would hit my watch when I said 'go' and hit it again when all thumbs were up. Then I would say something like, "Wow! You did that in 8.987 seconds. You've got the new world record!" I was just wearing a plain old watch—not a stop-watch—and the students never figured that out! They even began competing with my other classes to see if they could beat one another's times. They had me keep charts on the wall so that they could compare their times with my other classes! Oh, and they never tired of it!

Now here is a VERY important question: **Why did the students never tire of this procedure?** You'll probably be tempted to think the answer lies in the competition or the fun nature of the activity. Good guesses, but wrong. There's only one reason the students never tired of it: MY ENTHUSIASM! Every day, for every transition, I pretended I couldn't wait to see if they could beat their previous times. My excitement became theirs! Oh, and if I ever had (and I did) one student who did not participate in the activity, I pretended not to notice. Pick your battles carefully. Over the years, I have personally proven that the technique works in ALL grade levels. So give it a try. It's great fun, students love the idea, it adds excitement, and it saves time and aggravation. The record set by my class was 5.3245678932 seconds. I challenge you to beat that!

Students take their cues from you
So be enthusiastic.
YOUR excitement spills onto them.
The results? Nothing short of fantastic!

*If a student feels you're one he
can trust,
For trust, of course, is an
absolute must,
Then, from his mind, resistance
is freed
And now you can teach him.
You can teach him, indeed!*

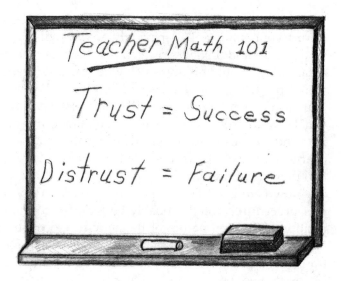

Put Students at Ease

Research has shown, time and again, that when we are feeling anxious or nervous, our brains begin to focus solely on ways to relieve the anxiety. Research also shows that **our brains take much longer to process a negative statement than to process a positive statement.** Well, we didn't even need the research to tell us that. Just think about it. When you're upset about something, it becomes your focus because you want to feel better. Not exactly rocket science! Now consider this one: If someone said, "Your hair looks nice today," you would probably thank the person and move on. It would feel nice to receive the compliment, but the compliment would not overtake your thinking. Conversely, if someone said, "Whatever look you were going for with your hair today, you missed!" you would most likely, after checking your hair in the mirror, feel upset. Then you would begin trying to figure out why they said what they said. You may even begin to experience a little righteous indignation. You might get angry, and anger sometimes leads to retaliation. But the fact is that no matter how hard you would try to let it go, your brain would want to focus on it for a while. It's a lot tougher to just *move on* when someone says something negative about you than it is when someone says something positive about you.

Okay, so what are the ramifications of this in the classroom? Again, it doesn't take a rocket scientist to understand that **in a negative environment—one where students are fearful, uncomfortable, and anxious—very little learning can take place** because all of those young brains are too busy focusing on trying to feel LESS fearful, LESS uncomfortable, and LESS anxious. You, as a teacher, can *nip this one in the bud* very easily and very early on. Here's how to do it: On the very first day of school, make it your number one priority to put your students at ease. Display a calm, composed demeanor. Make everything about you and your classroom say, "Welcome! I'm glad you're here." And then do one of the most important things you will do all year: Make promises to your students. **When you introduce yourself, begin NOT by telling them what you expect of them, but what <u>they</u> can expect of <u>you</u>.** Tell them about how exciting your class will be. Then make the following two promises to them:

1. **I will never raise my voice in this classroom.** That's right. I will not yell at you. That is not to say that I won't deal with misbehavior and hold you accountable, because I will. But I promise that I will deal with you in a private manner and treat each of you with respect. (Oh, and you don't have to add, "And I'll expect you to treat me with respect also," because students will automatically treat you with respect once they know you respect them!)

2. **I will never try to embarrass you in front of your peers.** So relax. You're safe here, and you're going to be amazed at how much we're all going to learn this year!

By making these two promises, you have accomplished two things:

1. **You have just made yourself accountable to your students.** Who better to hold you accountable? In case you don't yet know this, students will "hold you to your promises." And you'll lose their trust if you ever break a promise. So, basically, you've just taken the option of "losing your cool" away from yourself!

2. **You have managed to put your students at ease.** And when students are at ease, they will do their best; they will accept challenges; they will behave; they will succeed; and most importantly, they will never forget you for it!

Keep Me Busy

Busy, busy, you keep me busy
So much so, it makes me dizzy
Moving from one thing right to another
No time to think of anything other
Than the work I'm busy doing
Misbehavior has no time for brewing
Working, working all day long
No time for doing anything wrong
Questioning, answering, discovering,
    learning
There's an upward trend to the grades I'm
    earning
You keep me so busy and so engaged
I never have time to misbehave
Before I know it, the day is done
Learning, in your class, is really quite fun!
        A.L.B., 101 Poems for Teachers

Provide Structured "Bell-Work"

Why is it that some classrooms seem chaotic the second the students enter? And why is it that, in other classrooms, students enter and begin to work immediately? The simple answer is that **effective teachers know that they must have structured bell-work awaiting the students each day as they enter the classroom.** What is bell-work? Bell-work is an assignment that is posted in the same place every day for students to begin as soon as they walk into the room. The assignment is brief and interesting to the students, and it relates to the lesson that will be taught that day. Let's say that you will be discussing our country's justice system for the day's lesson. For the daily bell-work, you might have the following assignment posted:

> *Pretend that as of today, there are no more school rules. All students are free to do what they wish, with no limitations. Think about this for a minute, and then write three examples of realistic situations that could occur as a result of having no rules. Then, list three reasons you believe that rules are/are not necessary in this school.*

This bell-work assignment would take only a few minutes and would lead into a discussion of societal rules, laws, consequences, etc.

One of the keys to successful classroom management is to keep students actively involved from the moment they walk in until the moment they leave. **Remember: When you keep your students engaged and active, they can't find the time for behavior that's distractive!**

If I Could

If I could, then I would, whether or not
*   you think I should.*
I wouldn't because I couldn't; not
*   because you think I shouldn't.*
But I can't, so I won't, and since I won't
*   then I don't.*
Now should you feel confused, or should
*   you feel amused?*
Since you won't tell me what I should,
*   then I won't tell you, but I could!*

    A.L.B.

Avoid Power Struggles with Students

Effective teachers do not engage in power struggles with students, period! I was recently observing in a teacher's classroom when one of the students strutted in and announced to the class, "Guess what! My daddy won the lottery last night, and he said I can quit school, so good riddance to all of you!" I have to admit that I was amazed when the teacher simply looked at him, smiled, and said, "Boy, aren't you lucky!" and she immediately began teaching. The student had no *come-back* because he, too, was amazed and, I suppose, a little shocked. He simply went to his seat. I am quite certain that the student was attempting to provoke a struggle. However, it takes two people, and one wasn't playing. The teacher did not react, nor did she attack. And the story doesn't end there. The teacher later shared with me that the student stayed after class and apologized for his outburst.

Now consider the same scenario in the classroom of a teacher who engages in power struggles with students. It would have gone something like this:

Student: "Guess what! My daddy won the lottery last night, and he said I could quit school, so good riddance to all of you!"
Teacher: "First of all, young man, your daddy did not win the lottery because we would have heard about it. Also, you're not old enough to quit school. Don't ever come barging into my classroom like that again!"

Can you imagine where this could lead?

Again, effective teachers do not engage in power struggles with students. They **defuse the situation immediately by not providing the student with the desired response**, and they maintain their composure. Quite simply, they do not add fuel to the fire.

A struggle for power, a good teacher curtails, by removing the wind from a student's sails.

FACT: Logical consequences breed logical results! Illogical consequences breed illogical results!

Make the Punishment Fit the Misbehavior

I once watched a teacher punish a student who was talking out of turn. The punishment consisted of writing the entire text that he was supposed to be reading at the time of the misbehavior. I then thought to myself, "Wait a minute. This is a language arts teacher. Isn't she supposed to be instilling a love of reading and writing in these students? But isn't this punishment making the act of writing seem tedious and boring? Is she not turning this student off, fostering the same behavior for which she's punishing him?" There was no logic to this punishment. Following the lesson, I asked her about her choice of punishment and her desired result. She answered, "Well, I wanted for him to pay attention and to stop talking out of turn." "Did it work?" I asked. "No, not at all. He became quite defensive and refused to do the work. He threw his pencil aside and said he couldn't write all of that. Then he began talking again." "Why did you choose this particular punishment?" I asked. "I didn't know what else to do. His talking was aggravating me, so I just said the first thing that came to my mind." My suggestion to her was to try to make the punishment fit the misbehavior next time. She decided that a logical response to the misbehavior might have been to talk to him privately and let him know that his behavior was inappropriate and distracting to the other students. As a consequence, he would not be allowed to talk during the break between subjects, where students were allowed one minute of talking/stretching time.

The above scenario is a common one. **Teachers get frustrated, and they dole out illogical consequences**, saying things like, "If you don't stop it, you'll never see another recess." Or better yet, they make students write something like, "I will not talk out of turn," several hundred times. Where's the logic in that? There is none. Can you imagine being pulled over by a policeman who has had a frustrating day and decides to take your car away for a year as a punishment for having a broken headlight? Or can you imagine being caught doing what all teachers do—talking during a faculty meeting—and having to write, "I will not talk during faculty meetings," 500 times? These consequences are not logical, and they would only breed resentment. You do not want to breed resentment in students. Rather, you want to instill in them that rules are rules and they exist for a reason. If they choose to break a rule, then a logical consequence will follow.

Resist the temptation to let your level of frustration determine a punishment and its duration. Rather, make it clear that there's a consequence to an action, and a logical consequence will follow an infraction.

If you don't attack the problem and instead attack the person, the situation with that person will definitely worsen!

Attack the Problem, Not the Person

One of the biggest mistakes a teacher can make is to confuse the problem with the person. The two must be separated in order to truly deal with any problem or any person effectively. Let's make the concept simple. A student is consistently failing tests. You know that this student is quite capable. Attacking the person might sound like this: "Look, young lady, I know you're capable, and I want you to start putting forth some effort and pay attention in class. You should be making A's, but instead you're making F's. What's the matter with you?" Notice the sarcasm in the teacher's words and the blame placed upon the person. Also notice that the teacher, unaware of the cause of the problem, poses a *solution* for the student. Now let's consider the same scenario where the teacher attacks the problem instead of the person: "Rebecca, I notice that you're struggling with your grades. Knowing how capable you are, I'm concerned and was wondering if you could shed some light on what's going on. You seem to be distracted from your studies. Maybe I can help." Do you see the difference in the approach? Do you see how, in this scenario, the student's dignity is maintained, as the focus is on the problem and not the person? **It is human nature to defend against personal attack, and students are definitely human.**

One teacher summarized it quite well after I witnessed an interesting encounter she had with a student. The student walked into class very upset about something that had happened on the playground. She immediately began picking on another student in the classroom. The teacher asked her to be seated and the student retaliated with, "Leave me alone, you _____." (I'm sure you can fill in the expletive.) The teacher very calmly whispered something to the student, the student sat down, and the teacher began teaching, as if nothing had happened. After she got the class busy, she walked out with the student and had a private discussion. Following class, I said, "I was impressed with how calmly you handled that situation. I'm also curious as to what it was you said when you whispered to her and calmed her down." The teacher smiled and said, "Well, this student just moved here. So she doesn't know me well enough yet to determine whether I am a _____ or not. I may be, and I may not be, but she'll have to get to know me better before she can make such a statement. So I simply leaned over and explained what I just said to you. I told her that I would give her a few minutes to regain her composure and then we would deal with what had just happened. And of course, we did deal with it, and I learned a lot about that student in a little bit of time." I then asked, "Do you always handle such situations this calmly and professionally?" Once again, the teacher smiled and said, "I believe that if we, as teachers, really knew the faces behind the masks of some students, and if we understood what caused them to behave so inappropriately at times, and if we had any idea what struggles some of these students face, what cumbersome emotional loads some of them are carrying, then we would be heartbroken instead of angry." She followed that by saying, "Please understand that I don't excuse their behaviors. But my attitude and the beliefs that I just shared with you enable me to attack the problem instead of the person. I love those children, and whether they accept that love or not, I keep loving them anyway. Sooner or later, they all come around when they realize that I do care and that I won't attack." "How soon do you think this particular student will come around?" I asked. "She already did," replied the teacher. "How can you be sure?" I asked. "I just know," she said. "And it's the best feeling in the world!"

Problems with students take many disguises,
So do not attack the person when a problem arises.
Talk to the child and determine the problem's cause,
And help the child to solve the problem instead of attacking his flaws.

Planning

The Rewards of Planning

Coaches go into every game with a very specific plan
And surgeons plan their surgeries and proceed with a steady hand.
Attorneys defend their clients following much preparation
And players of chess only make a move after much deliberation.
Travelers go on vacation with their maps and proper clothing,
So why is it that some teachers speak of lesson plans with loathing?
The fact remains that failing to plan becomes a plan to fail.
You're a ship without an anchor, a hammer without a nail.
So plan your lessons every day,
Stay on the path so you won't go astray,
Know why you're teaching the things that you teach,
And reap your rewards from the students you reach.

A.L.B., *101 Poems for Teachers*

*There's only so much time in the day,
and not enough time to do it all.*

*There's no way to get what I need to get
done. What is sleep? I can't recall . . .*

Manage Your Time Wisely

A new teacher came into my office crying one day, saying, "I just can't do this. There aren't enough hours in the day." "Aren't enough hours in the day to do what?" I asked. "To be a teacher and still have a life—to grade papers, plan lessons, complete paperwork, and still manage to take care of my family at home. It's just not possible. I think I've chosen the wrong profession. My family is also beginning to suffer, because all I do is schoolwork, and I can't allow that to continue." I asked her to map out her day for me—her typical routine. It went like this:

- ◆ Wake up, and either grade a paper or two or spend a few minutes planning.
- ◆ Prepare breakfast, and try to grade another paper or two while eating.
- ◆ Get ready for school and get my child ready.
- ◆ Arrive at school, get a little more work done—usually while visiting with coworkers.
- ◆ Teach all day—with one hour of planning time, usually spent listening to the gripes of coworkers.
- ◆ Come home from school and spend all afternoon and evening trying to juggle cooking, cleaning, grading papers, planning lessons, doing homework with my child, etc.
- ◆ Cry myself to sleep in the wee hours of the morning!

I knew I had to help this teacher to develop some time management skills. What she was doing was running from one activity to the next, never really finishing one before she moved on to another. It would be overwhelming for any teacher to try to accomplish what she was attempting on such a schedule. So I made a simple suggestion that literally changed her life! I asked her how much focused time she had set aside every day to be completely alone with planning and paperwork. The answer, as you saw from her schedule, was none. I then asked if it would be possible to either come to school one hour earlier or stay one hour later—ALONE—in her classroom. She said she could come one hour earlier, because her husband took her child to school in the mornings. So we agreed that she would spend one hour, every morning, of uninterrupted planning time. We also *found* another hour during the day—her planning period. She agreed that instead of going into the teachers' lounge with her stack of paperwork, listening to and engaging in conversations with others, she would now spend that time in her room, alone.

The results? I received a phone call from the teacher. She said, "You saved my life! I'm sticking to my schedule, and it's working. I don't even have to take work home with me anymore. I have my life back. And I'm managing to stay on top of my planning, grading, and paperwork." She added, "Oh, and both my students and my family have noticed that I'm a much nicer and happier person!"

Remember: Schedule your time cleverly so that your workload is not so "heav'er'ly."

The fact that teaching is hard is outweighed by its reward!

Understand that Teaching Is Hard Work

"Oh, you're a teacher? Aren't you lucky! You get weekends off and tons of holidays and summers off and, wait, what time do you finish teaching every day? Wow! You've got it made!" Have you heard that yet? If not, you will. But I can guarantee you one thing: Whoever says that has never been a teacher! What that person or those people will never understand—so don't try to explain it, please—is that teaching is possibly the most demanding of all professions. It is also the most noble and rewarding!

Regrettably, many new teachers enter the profession with no concept of what will be required of them. They are often shocked to learn of all the paperwork and planning time involved, all the skills that are required to teach and manage a classroom effectively, all the patience, understanding and empathy they must possess, all the many hats they must wear, all the problems some students bring to school with them, etc.

Please understand that teaching is hard work! The road will be rocky at times. You will stumble and fall on occasion. You may even bleed a little. But remember that nothing worthwhile comes easily. The rewards of teaching far outweigh the demands. You will know this the first time you make a child smile, the first time you receive a sweaty hug, the first time you dry a student's tears on your shirt sleeve, the first time you open a present with crinkled wrapping paper and way too much tape, and any time you witness the slightest or greatest of achievements and the least or greatest of efforts from the children whose very lives you are helping to shape.

Yes, teaching is hard work. And the title *Teacher* is reserved only for those willing to rise to meet all of its many challenges, to give of themselves completely, and to be humble enough to accept, with dignity and grace, its tremendous responsibilities. If you are reading this, then you are very likely one of those chosen few.

I complained that my job was tough; I was a new teacher and it was rough,
But that all dissipated when outside my door a student waited
With a little present wrapped clumsily. It said, "Thank you, teacher, for loving me."

I'll Do it Tomorrow

I didn't feel like doing it, so I put it off for a day
And the next day came and I put off more—too
*   much was coming my way.*
I used up tons of paper with my list of "things
*   to do"*
And every day my "list of things" just grew
*   and grew and grew.*
It overtook my kitchen, then it overtook my
*   house.*
It overtook my children and it overtook my
*   spouse.*
If only I had done the things that needed to be
*   done,*
It would have been much easier to do things one by
*   one.*
But now I'm overwhelmed with all the things I did not do.
How will I survive this? I do not have a clue!
And sitting atop these things to do are feelings of guilt
*   and sorrow,*
So I'm turning over a new leaf. Yep, I'll do it tomorrow!
                           A.L.B., *101 Poems for Teachers*

Do Not Procrastinate

It happens to new teachers (and veterans) all the time—they enter into the "I'll do it tomorrow" cave. I call it a cave because it is a dark and scary place to live! Do NOT—I repeat—Do NOT go in there! It is alluring, I know. We all experience a sense of *overwhelm* from time to time, and it's easy to put one thing off. Then two things. Then three. And soon enough, you're swallowed by all you have to do, and there is no end in sight. It's that old familiar feeling of cramming for an exam the night before when we could have taken the smart route by studying over time, a little at a time. At least we could have passed the exam that way without a mental breakdown. I simply cannot stress enough how important it is that you, as a new teacher, do not allow yourself to procrastinate. Stay on top of your workload.

Simple FACT: It's much better to be on top of your workload than to have your workload on top of you! Don't put it off one more minute. Take a step right now. Begin it!

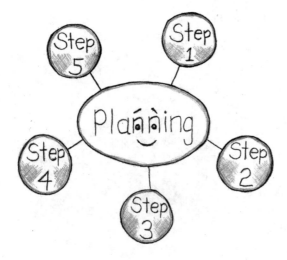

Failing to plan is just planning to fail
It's like trying to sail a sailboat that
doesn't have a sail . . .

Plan Effective Lessons

The very best teachers know that **if you want to *have* a great lesson, you have to *plan* a great lesson**. It truly is that simple. But understand that planning takes time. However, if you teach a well-planned lesson, then you can really enjoy your teaching. Now, does that mean that you will accomplish everything you intend to accomplish or that your plan will go off without a hitch? Of course not. Teaching is not an exact science, and that is why we need to plan so thoroughly.

Teachers who do not plan good lessons end up struggling with behavior problems, off-task students, and general chaos. In order for the students to learn a new skill, the lesson must be well thought-out and well taught. Good planning is a skill; and it requires training, patience, practice, and guidance. Mentors can play a critical role by spending time planning with new teachers.

The following are some simple tips for you to use when planning any lesson:

- Determine your objective.
- Decide how you will make the lesson interesting and inviting for your students.
- Be sure to make an effort to actively involve your students in every part of the lesson.
- Plan to state the lesson's purpose, relate the skill to students' real lives, teach and model the skill, practice the skill with them, have them try the new skill independently, and review.
- Gather any necessary materials beforehand.
- Enjoy teaching your well-planned lesson!

Any teacher who plans all lessons and activities following the above steps will see instant results from students.

If you plan your lessons with careful attention
And treat each one as a special invention
You're sure to see student success and retention
Reducing your levels of stress and tension!

Tip from Breaux, A. & Whitaker, T. (2006). *Seven Simple Secrets: What the BEST Teachers Know and Do!* Larchmont, NY: Eye On Education.

My classroom was a place of disgrace, so messy I couldn't see each student's face
So I found a place for everything and put everything in its place
And now my room's a wonderful space where teaching and learning always take place.

Be Organized and Prepared

Imagine walking into a doctor's office where you come in on two legs and walk out on crutches due to tripping on some of the mess on the floor. Imagine going into a courtroom where the judge can't find his gavel, the jury is walking around and talking, there's paper strewn all over the floor, and the attorneys keep having to stop so that they can run out to their cars to find some of their missing evidence. Would you feel like you're being treated fairly in either of these scenarios? Likewise, students are not being treated fairly in disorderly classroom environments.

Organization is not a skill that comes naturally or easily to some. However, it is a skill that MUST be acquired if you desire to be an effective teacher. An organized room gives the message that the teacher is competent and well prepared. And in organized environments, students tend to be more organized, more respectful of the classroom property, more respectful of the teacher, and better behaved. Students want and need structure. They want a teacher who is well prepared and well organized. Knowing where everything is—a place for everything, and everything in its place—makes for a calmer environment. I have often noticed that when classrooms are in disarray and the teacher is running from here to there trying to locate materials during the lesson or trying to fill in with something to keep the students busy because the lesson was not well prepared, the students tend to mimic that behavior.

The bottom line is this: If your classroom is an ordered, highly functional place, the students will be much more likely to mimic that environment. And when teachers are organized and prepared, there is very little, if any, time for off-task behavior. The class runs very smoothly, from bell to bell. Procedures are established, materials are readily available, the room is not cluttered or dirty, the lessons flow very smoothly, and the whole environment is that of a safe, orderly, inviting place to learn.

Now let's look at the other side of that. I walked into a teacher's classroom some time back, and I couldn't believe my eyes. There was *stuff* everywhere. Student projects were all over the floor, the desks just seemed to be scattered around, there were stacks of books and papers everywhere, the teacher's desk looked like it had been struck by a tornado, and there was garbage that *hadn't quite made it* lying beside the garbage can. The teacher, flustered, was literally running between activities trying to find this worksheet or that lesson plan or some textbook. The students were out of their desks, talking, roaming about. One student actually tripped on one of many obstructions in the aisle. For one solid hour, I can say that I witnessed no actual teaching and learning. Everyone just sort of blended in with the mess. In one word: chaos. The teacher apologized for the mess and jokingly said, "The custodian won't even come in here to clean." Needless to say, we saw to it that she received some guidance from her mentor and from a few other willing teachers who agreed to spend a Saturday helping her to get organized. Though things are not completely ordered yet, she has come a long way. A visit to her classroom after she became better organized revealed the following:

♦ Teaching and learning taking place
♦ Better student behavior
♦ Better student participation
♦ Much less off-task behavior
♦ A calmer environment
♦ A more positive environment

Again, students need structured, ordered, welcoming environments. And it is important that they see their teacher as a true professional—one who is always prepared and who structures the class so that lessons flow, students are kept busy, and no one's life is at risk amid the chaos!

Disarray keeps learning away, so just say YES and clean up that MESS!

One record, two records, three records, four
Grade records, attendance records, portfolios and more
By tracking student progress, you can help your students soar
And you can use the data to help you find new teaching techniques to explore!

Maintain Accurate Records

In this day and age, we hear so much about accountability and the importance of maintaining accurate and thorough records on each of our students. "What if a parent sues us because he refuses to believe that his child can do any wrong?" "With statewide testing of students, will I lose my job if my students don't score well?" "I witnessed the fight, and I documented everything I saw—just in case there's a lawsuit." The list goes on and on. And though I am in no way implying that these are not real and important issues, I choose not to focus on these issues here. Rather, I choose to focus on the importance of maintaining accurate records for the sake of improving student achievement and providing parents and key educators involved in each child's education with the information they need to do just that—improve each child's education. I believe that the day that I begin tracking student progress and behavior out of "fear" is the day that I should leave the teaching profession.

So what benefits are there for students if a teacher maintains accurate records? The benefits are simple: Improved teaching and learning! I was called into a school recently to help deal with a "problem" child. The child had two teachers, only one of whom was having difficulties with him, so I decided to acquire input from both. When I spoke with the first teacher and asked her to tell me about Thomas, she responded, "Let me get my grade book and I'll show you his grades." In the grade book, next to Thomas's name, were all failing grades on all graded assignments. I then asked the teacher to tell me about Thomas's strengths. She responded, "He has no real strengths, as you can see from his grades." "What does he struggle with most?" I asked. "Everything," she responded. "He won't behave, and he refuses to put any effort into his schoolwork." I asked if she had work samples, behavior records, documentation of anything she was doing to improve the situation, etc. The only things she could produce were several test papers with big fat red F's on them—no comments, nothing. I then asked what types of unique approaches she was taking or strategies she was using to accommodate his specific needs. Once again, she could give me nothing. I thought to myself, "How can you accommodate a student's needs if you don't even know what his needs are?" There was no doubt in my mind as to why Thomas was *drowning* in this teacher's classroom. I then moved on to the next teacher. Not only did she provide me with a grade book, but she presented a portfolio of his work, letters of communication with his father, a picture of him from a bulletin board, a letter that he had written to her, a chart on his behavior, samples of graded assignments on which she had written lots of comments (most of which were positive, and all of which were constructive). And last, but definitely not least, there were teacher notes that specified unique approaches and strategies she used to teach Thomas, with red asterisks next to those that were most successful. Not surprisingly, Thomas, though not making straight A's, posed no problems, academically or behaviorally, in this teacher's classroom. She went on to tell me, without my asking, about all of Thomas's strengths: his outgoing personality, his leadership qualities, his creativity, and his determination to succeed, especially when things did not come easily to him. Was this the same Thomas? Yes, but I would have never known it by listening to the two "eye witness" accounts! Same Thomas, different teachers. You decide.

Bottom line: **Effective teachers maintain accurate records in order to track student progress, to search for patterns in student learning and behavior, to adjust teaching accordingly, and to communicate effectively with parents.** Needless to say, the lives of all the "Thomases" are profoundly affected.

Effective teachers maintain accurate documentation
To lessen their own and their students' frustration
And they don't just collect it, but they use the information
To help them in their lesson and strategy formation
Because effective teachers have only one destination
Successful students—an effective teacher's jubilation!

Without a destination, you'll experience
desperation
For you'll never know when you get there;
you could be there right now...
But where is 'there' when you're not aware?
Confusing, bemusing? And how!

Make the Objectives "Clear" for Each Lesson

"What did you learn in school today?" ask many parents when their children return home. "I don't know," answer far too many children. "Well, what did you do?" ask the parents. "Well, we had to write a lot and read some stories and read a chapter and answer the questions at the end of the chapter and fill out a lot of stupid worksheets!" Okay, so now we know what they did, but we still don't know what they learned! Therefore, we must ask the question here, "Does a teacher who engages students in the aforementioned activities have clear objectives for each lesson, and does the teacher make those objectives known to the students?"

Imagine going on a vacation and having no destination. How would you know what to pack? Imagine a doctor performing surgery without an objective. "Oh well, I'll just open him and take a look around and see what's what!" Or imagine being the patient, knowing you'll be undergoing surgery, but you have no idea why! I know, it seems ridiculous. But it's just as ridiculous for students to be unclear on exactly what it is they're supposed to be accomplishing.

Simply stated, **an objective defines what the students should know or be able to do at the end of each lesson.** I've often watched teachers tell students to read a chapter and answer the questions at the end of the chapter when they're finished. The students reluctantly get busy, but they have no idea *why* they have to do this. In fact, it's a good rule to know that when students ask, "Why do we have to do this?" it's like a red flag reminding you that you have obviously forgotten to make the objective for the lesson clear. It goes without saying that you, the teacher, must write clear, measurable objectives for every lesson you teach. But that's not enough. You must now make the objectives clear to your students. Make it a point, as you begin each lesson, to tell your students, "Guess what you'll be able to do at the end of this lesson," and then tell them. That way, here's what you'll get:

You'll know where you're going; students will know what they're learning, their knowledge will be growing, and better grades they will be earning!

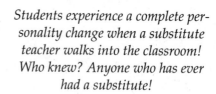

Thank you!

Students experience a complete personality change when a substitute teacher walks into the classroom! Who knew? Anyone who has ever had a substitute!

Provide a Plan for Substitutes

As a new teacher, I made many mistakes, mostly due to lack of experience. One of the biggest mistakes I made was not realizing that my students, in my absence, would take advantage of a substitute teacher. The story goes like this:

It was my first year of teaching, and I had to attend a meeting. It was going to be the first day of school that I had ever missed. Still wearing my rose-colored glasses and never having left my seventh graders in the hands of a substitute teacher, I never anticipated what "could" and probably "would" happen during my absence. I thought I had all of my bases covered. I had left explicit instructions for the substitute teacher—down to the last detail. I told my students I would be out, that a substitute teacher would be with them, and that I would see them the day after. By this time, I had my classroom management system well organized. My students knew what I expected, and they followed all of my procedures beautifully. So I had nothing to worry about. Right? Oh, how very wrong! I returned the following day to learn that my little "angels" had turned into raging devils in the hands of the substitute. The substitute vowed never to come near my class again. She was devastated, and so was I. How could this have happened? What had gone wrong? I learned the hard way that I had missed one crucial step. Yes, I had provided the substitute teacher with explicit instructions, but I had totally forgotten about the instructions for my students. So just as the poor, unsuspecting substitute teacher vowed never to enter my classroom doors again, I vowed never to let such a situation occur again should I be absent. The solution was quite simple, and it worked like a charm! The next time I had a meeting to attend, this is what I did, step by step:

- ◆ I told my students I would be absent and that I would need for them to take over the classroom and help the substitute teacher. I made a big deal over that fact that I knew I could trust them, so I was not at all worried about whether or not things would run smoothly.

- I assigned roles to each student. For instance, one student had the task of welcoming the substitute and showing her where everything was located on my desk. Another student had the job of handing out the bell-work assignment to students as they entered the classroom. Another student had the job of giving the signal for quiet when the substitute was ready to begin and sharing that same signal with the substitute so that she could use it also. Another student had the job of explaining all of the daily procedures to the substitute. Another had the job of picking up assignments from students as they finished their work. I kept creating "jobs" until every student had one. One student even had the job of presenting the substitute with a small gift to show their appreciation at the end of the class period. Another had the job of "beginning the applause" after the gift was given. All students shared the job of thanking the substitute on the way out of the classroom, and one student was assigned to remind any student who forgot. Okay, you get the picture.

- On the day before I was to be absent, we practiced by pretending that I was the substitute. The students loved the idea, because now they were in charge of running the classroom and helping to make things easy on the substitute teacher. They had specific responsibilities, and they took pride in that fact.

- I wrote down all responsibilities of every student, and each got a copy. This would help to ensure that they would hold each other accountable or simply remind each other if one of them forgot his assigned job.

- We also discussed the fact that this same plan would remain in place if I were ever absent due to illness. For this, we kept an extra "gift" in the closet.

Results? I returned the day after my absence to find a two-page letter from the substitute. She said to PLEASE call her if I ever needed a substitute again. She went on to say that she had never witnessed anything like it. She was amazed at how helpful and cooperative the students were. "And can you believe that they actually clapped for me at the end of the class? I've never received applause in my life! And I believe that every single one of them stopped to thank me on the way out." You see, the students had played their roles so well that she didn't even realize that most of it had been rehearsed and that they were *supposed* to stop and thank her on the way out.

The students couldn't wait to brag about how well they had run the class without me! It worked for me every time I used it over the years, and I even used it with a college class just to prove that the technique was not specific to any grade or age level. It will work for you, too!

Don't be scared when a substitute comes. Just let the students ensure the classroom hums like the well-oiled machine that works when you're there. How do you do this? Prepare, prepare, prepare!

Instruction

Make It Real

I just don't see the point in why I need to know this junk
You say if I don't learn it, then surely I will flunk
But I need a better reason for learning all this stuff
It's boring and it's pointless, so learning it is rough
And every time I'm bored in school, I think of other things
Lost inside a daydream until the school bell rings
Which means I haven't learned it, which means my grades are bad
Which means that I'm in trouble and my mom and dad are mad
And then I get so far behind that it's just too late to pass
So next year here I am again—I'm right back in your class
I didn't get it last year; I don't get it today
Please, teacher, make it real for me so that I can move on in May!

A.L.B., *Seven Simple Secrets*

*Our greatest glory is not in never
falling, but in rising every time we fall.*
Confucius

Learn to Recover Quickly

One of the biggest mistakes that new teachers make is being afraid to ask for help for fear of appearing *stupid*. Well, here are a few facts:

♦ New teachers are not supposed to know it all.

♦ Veteran teachers are not supposed to know it all.

♦ No one knows it all.

♦ Anyone who acts like a "know-it-all" is attempting to hide the fact that they don't know much of anything!

Teachers, even the best of them, make mistakes. We are, after all, human. One of the differences between effective teachers and ineffective teachers is that effective teachers know how to recover from their mistakes quickly. When they make a mistake, they readily admit it. If at all possible, they correct it. And then they move on. Ineffective teachers try to hide behind defensiveness, thus making the mistake a bigger deal than it usually is and preventing themselves from earning the respect of their students.

When you say something you should not have said, when you inadvertently hurt a child's feelings, when you give incorrect information, etc., apologize immediately and correct the mistake if possible. Acknowledge your mistake and then let it go. By doing this, you will earn the respect of those you work with and those you teach, and you will be teaching others that mistakes, if handled appropriately, can provide wonderful opportunities for learning and growing.

*When you make a mistake, don't be defensive or fake
Just admit your mistake and then attempt to learn from it
You'll fall but won't break, so get up and overcome it!*

Teach Students at "Their Level"

I have always been baffled by the age-old questions asked time and again by educators: "At what level should we teach students? Should we teach them at their own level or at grade level?" Well, think about this: When you first learned to speak, you learned at YOUR level. It didn't matter that other babies your age spoke sooner or later than you did. You had to be ready. You couldn't have possibly learned to speak at anyone else's level. So you learned at your level, and today you can speak. When you learned to walk, it was at YOUR level. It didn't matter that some babies walked as early as seven months and you did not walk until thirteen months. No one panicked. They simply waited until you were ready. You learned at your level, and today you can walk. And so it went for any skill you learned as you were growing up—that is, until you got to school. Then you were possibly expected to read before you were ready, which, of course, is impossible—but hey, lots of other kids your age could do it. And if you were forced to attempt skills at levels above your own, then you experienced failure, which, of course, bred more failure. **The simple fact is that none of us can learn anything at anyone else's level.** However, if we are taken from our level and moved forward, one step at a time, then there's no stopping us!

I have had the privilege of knowing, for many years, a teacher who believes that students must be taught at their own levels. She teaches in a middle school where the population is impoverished and most of the students are considered *at risk*. Her students consist of *alternative* students—seventh graders who have been retained as many as three times, many of whom are 15 years old. Her task is to teach, in one school year, both the seventh and eighth grade curriculums to these students in order to prepare them for the eighth grade statewide criterion-referenced test. If they pass the test, they move on to the ninth grade. Now remember that these students are considerably behind *typical* seventh graders in their achievement. The task seems insurmountable, and most teachers would say it's impossible. Are you ready for the results? This teacher's students have almost a 90% passing rate on the statewide test. In fact, their passing rate is above both the district and the state levels! How does this teacher do it? How does she take students who have trouble writing complete sentences and get them to write structured essays within less than eight months? Her answer? "I teach them at their own levels. If they can't write a sentence, even though they're *supposed* to be able to write sentences at their age,

I simply teach them how to write a sentence. When they're ready, we move on to writing paragraphs and then eventually essays. I make sure that they experience nothing but success, and it becomes a habit—a way of thinking."

I guess it is true that "common sense is not necessarily common." If all teachers took all students from where they were and moved them forward to where they could be (as opposed to teaching them at the level they're "supposed" to be), the student achievement in our nation's schools would skyrocket!

Remember, we teach STUDENTS. And the only way to teach students is AT THEIR LEVELS!

Teach me at my level, for that is where I revel
My behavior, then, might be more of an angel than a devil
And once success is mine, there will be no stopping me
So teach me at my level and achievement's what you'll see!

By watching other teachers in action
Without having my own class as a distraction
I can see what works and what does not
By observing others, I can learn a lot!

Observe Other Teachers

When I graduated from college, I went straight into my own classroom. That classroom is where I lived, basically. I met my coworkers, but I never had the privilege of seeing them teach. I did ask lots of questions of them, and they were always happy to share their secrets and their wisdom. However, I never got to see them in action. Then, one day, my eyes were opened. I was placed on a committee whose job was to observe all of the teachers in a neighboring school who were currently implementing a particular program. For the first time since I began teaching, I actually got to observe other teachers teaching. It was wonderful! I learned so much in that one day. In the effective teachers' classrooms, I learned better ways of dealing with students—behaviorally and academically. In less effective teachers' classrooms, I learned a lot about what not to do. But in all of the classrooms, I LEARNED and I instantly became a better teacher!

Teaching continues to be a very "isolated" profession. We spend the majority of our time in our own classrooms and rarely see beyond our four walls! Yet **collaboration has proven time and again to be very beneficial, rejuvenating, and enlightening for teachers.** So why don't we do more of it? Some of our best ideas are "stolen" from other teachers. And the good news is that teachers are a very generous group of people, always happy to share their successes with others. Ask teachers how many opportunities they have had to observe other teachers teaching and they will tell you that these opportunities have either been rare or nonexistent. If you are a mentor, don't just observe the teacher you are mentoring. Allow that teacher to learn from observing you and others. Just as it's crucial that as teachers we model the skills we teach our students, so must mentors model good teaching for the teachers they're mentoring. **If you are a new teacher, ask your administrator to schedule some time for you to observe your mentor and others.** You'll be amazed at how much you will learn from watching others. Oh, and don't sell yourself short. Your mentor will also be amazed at how much there is to learn from watching you!

Teach, teach, teach away
Preach, preach all the day
You'd save your voice and I'd learn more, too
If you'd stop talking and let me do!

Refrain from Lecturing

Parent: What did you learn in school today?
Child: I learned swimming.

Parent: They taught you to swim?
Child: No, they taught me swimming.

Parent: So you can swim now?
Child: No, but I know swimming. Ask me any question you want about swimming.

Parent: The only important question is, "Can you swim?"

FACT: Lecturing is the one of the LEAST effective means of instructing, yet it is the most often used! To make that point clear, let's imagine that you are learning a new skill—you are learning to swim. Your instructor seats you and twenty other novices in desks beside the pool. He lectures to you on swimming and you take notes. You literally hear everything there is to know about swimming because your instructor is an advanced swimmer. He knows his stuff! All of his information is accurate, so you are receiving "good" instruction. In fact, he even gets into the pool and models good swimming for you. After memorizing everything there is to know about swimming, you take the exam: a written test. You have put much time and effort into your studies, and you ace the exam. You are now a good swimmer. Right??? WRONG! We don't learn to swim by listening to great lectures on swimming. We learn to swim by swimming. We don't learn to drive a car by listening to informative lectures on driving. We learn by actually "doing" the driving. So it is in life, and so it is in the classroom. That is not to say that there is never a place for lecturing, but lecturing does not teach us to *do* anything. Great writers did not become great writers because they listened to lectures and memorized all of the *rules*. Good readers did not become good readers by listening to lectures on reading. They became adept at their skills through *doing*. Great historians did not become great historians by listening to lectures and memorizing history. They actually dove in and swam around in history. I've often heard it said, "The one who does the doing does the learning." I have yet to hear it said that the one who can listen really intently to great lectures does the learning. Perhaps I missed that particular lecture!

You lecture, lecture, lecture and I cannot listen to it
Do you really want me to learn it? Then let me attempt to DO IT!

I know of no adults who owe their successes to the efficacy of a textbook, but of many who owe their successes to the influence of a teacher...

Refrain from "Textbook Teaching"

No, I am not suggesting that you throw away your trusty textbooks. I can think of very few teachers who do not use textbooks. Textbooks are valuable resources. Ah, that is the key—they are *resources*. I witnessed a conversation in a faculty lounge that went like this: "Can you believe that they've adopted this new textbook? I can't teach from that. I'm going to continue to use the textbook I've been using. I'm not about to change all of my lesson plans because of a new textbook. Also, this textbook has too much material to cover in one school year. I can cover the textbook I'm using now in exactly one school year." This brought to mind another teacher who used to have his students, on the first day of school, actually *sit* on their textbooks. He would then say, "Okay, we have now *covered* the textbook." This is not to say that he did not use the textbook. He did. But he used it as a supplement to his teaching. The textbook did not make his instructional decisions. He made his instructional decisions based on the needs of his students. So should we all. Most districts have very specific curriculums, and no textbook has an exact correlation to any district's curriculum. However, when selecting textbooks, districts consider those that have the closest correlation to their curriculums. Often, however, teachers see the textbook as the definitive curriculum. They cover the book from beginning to end, neglecting to teach much of the district's curriculum. **The effective teacher begins with the curriculum and then determines the best resources available to teach that curriculum.** The ineffective teacher depends on textbooks to tell him what to teach, when to teach it, what questions to ask, what answers the students should give, and to provide him with formatted tests and answer keys to everything he has *covered*. Ask yourself, "If all of the textbooks were removed from my classroom, would I be able to continue my teaching?" If your answer is *no*, then you are relying too heavily on the textbook in your instruction. Remember, textbooks are resources. We teach students, not textbooks.

Think about this very hard, even though it's scary,
If textbooks can teach students, then you're unnecessary!

Right

Wrong

If people had better social skills, there would be fewer social ills.

Teach Social Skills

Assume nothing! Don't expect students to come to you with perfect manners, to know right from wrong, to work cooperatively with others. Some will, but many won't. I often hear it said that parents should be responsible for teaching social skills. I'm not arguing that point. But the fact remains that **many students learn good social skills from their parents and many do not.** So where do we find time to *fit it in* to the overloaded curriculum? We begin by being good models. And then we weave social skills into everything we teach. I knew a teacher who complained about her students having no manners or social skills. When I asked how she incorporated social skills into her teaching, she said, "I don't. It's not my job." Upon observing her, I noticed that not only did she refrain from teaching social skills, but she also refrained from modeling them. She was loud, she displayed negative body language, she never said *please* or *thank you*, and her lessons were boring. Students worked alone, and it's tough to learn social skills without the benefit of social interaction! Out of curiosity, I observed the same students with another teacher. Guess what! They were no longer ill-behaved. This teacher greeted her students with a smile; she thanked them often; she took time, when introducing a group activity, to discuss proper behavior; and she basically did the exact opposite of the first teacher. Thus, she got opposite behavior!

I went back to the first teacher and said, "I agree that your students are a little lacking in social skills." "A little lacking?" she asked. "Try ground zero!" "Okay," I said. "I'm going to help you to turn that around, if you're willing." "Sure," she said. "I'll try anything." Without telling her what I had observed in the other teacher's classroom, I simply gave her a list of what the other teacher was doing. I had her do five things: 1) greet students every day as if you are happy to see them, 2) speak with a pleasant tone, and don't lose your temper at any cost, 3) thank your students for appropriate behavior, 4) explain what proper behavior looks like well in advance of activities, and 5) allow more student interaction.

I observed her for five days. Following each observation, I provided feedback, and we discussed changes in student behavior. By the end of the week, she was a new person, and her students were different students. To this day, she thanks me for helping her to change. She has never said, "Thanks for helping my students to behave." Instead, she realizes that SHE made the difference.

Display the behaviors you'd like to see, and students will respond readily. For students emulate what you do, so the lessons you 'model' will stick like glue!

Point out all my weaknesses, and those are all you'll see,
But find one strength, acknowledge it, and better I might be…

Focus on Students' Strengths

Quick activity: Think of two of your most challenging students. Get them clearly in your mind. Now list ten strengths and ten weaknesses of each. Was it easier to come up with the weaknesses? If so, you are not alone. Most teachers are far more adept at spotting student weaknesses than they are at identifying student strengths. But knowing that success truly does breed success, **we need to turn our thinking around and begin focusing on the strengths of each student.** A teacher once insisted to me that she had three students who made her entire life miserable. I asked her to tell me about the strengths of each, and she answered, "None of them have any strengths." No wonder these students were causing problems in the classroom. They were considered "hopeless" in the eyes of their teacher. **The fact is that every student possesses lots of strengths.** At times, we have to search a little harder and dig a little deeper to find strengths in some, but the strengths are there.

I observed these three students, all of whom happened to be boys, in this teacher's classroom, and then I followed the three boys into another teacher's classroom. Seeing that these students experienced *personality* changes in the second teacher's classroom, I decided to speak to the second teacher. I asked her to tell me about each boy, listing his strengths and weaknesses. Her comments were: "Wendell is very polite. He does struggle with the content, but he gives 100% in effort. He has wonderful leadership abilities, and he has a heart of gold. His penmanship is meticulous, and his work is always done so neatly. He's also a very good listener." The comments about the other two boys were very similar in that they focused on strengths as opposed to weaknesses. I then asked the teacher what she did differently with Wendell, since he had trouble grasping the content. She answered, "I provide remediation activities, and then he catches on because he's so wiling and determined. I also give him lots of responsibilities around the classroom because he handles responsibility very well. I just do things that help to ensure his success every day, and the growth in him has been phenomenal!" Wow! What a difference! Same students. Different teachers. You decide.

If you really want your students to succeed, then focus on their strengths, indeed. By pointing out what each does well, difficult behavior you soon will quell!

Cooperation

*When people work together, there's
no storm they can't weather
The workload is lightened and
achievement is heightened
Their smiles are brightened and
they appear more enlightened
So teach the children that cooperation is the key
And cooperation is what you soon
will see!*

A.L.B.

Allow and Encourage Students to Work Cooperatively

It is often stated that any teacher who argues against encouraging students to work cooperatively has never encouraged students to work cooperatively. Life is about cooperation. We simply cannot expect students to come to us possessing all of the skills they need in order to work cooperatively with others. That's why they need us! We're here to teach them.

Much research has been conducted on the power of cooperative learning. The results have been consistent: **Students who engage in cooperative learning activities develop problem-solving skills, develop better social skills, and achieve at higher levels.** So why is it that so many teachers, of all grade levels, tend to avoid the idea of having students work together in cooperative learning environments? Once again, we must look back at classroom management. The following are actual teachers' answers to the question, "Why don't you use cooperative learning activities in your classroom?"

- I've tried letting my students work together, and they just can't get along with one another.
- I put my students in groups, and one person does all of the work.
- I don't want to hold back the stronger students because of the weaker students.
- Cooperative learning equals chaos. I want structure and order in my classroom.
- Today's students simply cannot work together.
- I tried cooperative learning once, and my students argued with one another.
- I like a quiet classroom. I'm not about to put my students in groups where all they'll do is talk.

Notice that in all of the above answers, the issues of order, structure, noise, lack of on-task behavior, and chaos are evident. Again, **all point to problems in classroom management**. Yes, the above fears can become realities, but NOT with true cooperative learning conducted in a well-managed environment. The key here is structure. It is impossible to do justice to describing cooperative learning completely here. However, I will provide enough of the overall premise underlying the success of its use in the classroom to encourage those reading this to familiarize themselves with some of the literature on cooperative learning. In a nutshell, this is what true cooperative learning looks like:

♦ Students are assigned to groups consisting of various personality types and ability levels.

♦ Each student in the group has a specific job in carrying out the overall charge of the group.

♦ All activities are highly structured.

♦ Appropriate behaviors in the group are taught, modeled, and practiced.

♦ Noise levels are under control, and all "noise" is "structured" noise.

♦ Students of all ability levels are challenged to think critically and to solve problems cooperatively, just like in the real world.

♦ Procedures for each aspect of group interaction are clearly established, from day one.

♦ Students are involved in the group's mission, and they experience high levels of success.

Remember that before implementing any type of cooperative group activities, effective classroom management must be in place.

Question: Do your students know how to work together—to cooperate with one another? If not, it's time to teach them.

Why Do We Have to Know This?

"Why do we have to know this?" asked the student,
looking confused.
His classmates echoed his sentiments and their
teacher was not amused,
But the fact remains that people learn best when they
know what they're learning and WHY,
So connect what you teach to your students' real
lives, and watch them succeed and comply!

A.L.B.

Relate Lessons to Real Life

If you are a new teacher, just starting out, with a long, successful career of teaching ahead of you, then I will go out on a limb here and assume you're not interested in attending the meeting this afternoon for soon-to-be teacher retirees. If your savings account is a little on the shallow end of the pool, I'll assume you're not currently researching where to invest hundreds of thousands of dollars. Right? These topics are of no interest to you because you simply cannot relate to them.

Aristotle said, "All knowledge is relational." In other words, in order for us to learn anything new, we must have something we already "know" with which to connect the new skill. When work makes sense to us, we have a purpose for doing it. If it does not seem meaningful, we close our minds to it. After all, **what's the point in learning something that has no meaning in our lives?** I often hear students say that they *hate* English or they *hate* reading. However, I am yet to encounter students who *hate* English or reading when it comes to reading the menu at their favorite fast-food restaurant or when they receive a note from a friend or when they want to browse through the television listings.

Let's drive this point home with a classroom experience that most, if not all, of us have had. We all learned about *nouns* in a similar fashion. In fact, our experiences were so similar, no matter where we went to school, that it's almost frightening. It went like this:

> *The teacher began the lesson by saying, "Open your English books to page 27."*
> *We all sighed, as though we were being tortured. At the top of the page it said,*
> *"Nouns." We had to copy that title into our notebooks. Then we had to copy the*
> *definition that said, "A noun names a person, place, or thing." Then we categorized*
> *people, places, and things. Next we did Exercise A where we had to underline the*
> *nouns. Following Exercise A, we did Exercise B. We did the worksheet on nouns*
> *after that.*

What did any of this have to do with our actual lives other than the fact that we may have wanted to pass the test, which was, of course, on Friday? That, by the way, is NOT a real-life connection! Is it any wonder that students claim to hate English or any other subject that is taught in this fashion?

Now let's consider a completely different scenario. Notice that it takes no extra time or work. It simply involves asking yourself the question that all great teachers ask themselves when planning any lesson: "How does this particular skill or piece of knowledge affect the lives of my students today?"

> *The teacher begins the lesson by saying, "You don't need to take a thing out right now. Angela, tell me about something you did yesterday, but do not name any people, any places, or any things." Angela says, "My brother and..." And the teacher interrupts and says, "Oops, your brother is a person." Then she says, "went to the mall..." and the teacher interrupts and says, "No, the mall is a place." And Angela is having difficulty. The teacher then asks another student to help by telling something he did yesterday, without, of course, naming any people, places, or things. Within seconds, the students figure out that the task is impossible. The teacher says, "Oh, so you're telling me that without people, places, and things, you cannot speak in a way that makes sense? Okay, then write a sentence about something you did yesterday without naming any people, places, or things." As the students get busy, the teacher walks around and has each student cross out any word that is a person, place, or thing. When everyone has finished, they begin to share their sentences. Tim reads his. It sounds like this: "A it the at the in the." The students laugh and realize that writing makes no sense either without including people, places, or things. The teacher then says, "So you're telling me that you could not speak or write or even THINK without people, places, and things? They're called nouns, by the way. Okay, so how would your life be different if nothing you said made sense to anyone anymore? A discussion follows as to the importance of these parts of speech—nouns.*

Do you see how the teacher has gotten the students to understand the real-life connection and its importance in their everyday lives? That's teaching! Afterward, if the teacher chooses to use the textbook definition and to have the students complete exercises A and B, that is fine, as the relevance of what they're doing has been established! I'll bet that some of you reading this are thinking to yourself, "I've never even thought about nouns that way before!" That's because it was never taught to you in that way, so you never really stopped to analyze the importance of every facet of our language.

How can we, as teachers, expect our students to *buy in* to something for which they see no meaning? We can't! So make that real-life connection with every skill you teach. And if you ever come across a skill that truly has no real-life connection, then we should remove that skill from the curriculum! Oh, and the infamous question, "Why do we have to know this?" is a RED FLAG to you that you have not made that critical *real-life* connection!

Making it REAL has tremendous APPEAL!

The Life of a Kid

Go to school all the day
Do your homework before you play
Be sure to be in bed by eight
Up at dawn, do not be late
Tonight inside my bed I lay
A very selfish prayer I pray
I beg and plead with Mr. Sun
Shine longer tomorrow—
I need to have fun.

A.L.B., *101 Poems for Teachers*

Avoid Homework Overload

Parents complain about homework, children complain about homework, and teachers complain about how their students do not turn in homework. **No one seems to be too crazy about the idea of homework, yet some teachers keep piling it on.** Imagine if a student has six teachers and each assigns homework activities that require twenty minutes of work. That's two hours, IF the student understands the concepts and does not struggle. Where does he find time to be a child? Also, many students are involved in after-school activities. Is it any wonder that parents get upset and many students do not turn in their homework assignments?

As the saying goes, "Everything in moderation." Students spend between seven and eight hours a day at school. Does it make sense to send them home with hours of work? If I work hard every day with my students, then homework should not be a nightly event. Much controversy has arisen involving *homework* questions. Do students need homework? Does it improve achievement? Does it foster responsibility? Should it affect student grades? To date, the jury is still out on the homework issue.

I am not opposed to homework, but my suggestions to you are as follows:

1. Assign it only in moderation.

2. Make any homework assignments interesting and doable.

3. Remember that the old trick of doubling the homework if they don't do it has never worked. (If they didn't do it once, they won't do it twice!)

4. Remember that many students do not have the luxury of parental help with homework.

5. Remember that we teach children, and children need to be children. For that matter, let's hope there's a little bit of a child left in all of us. If we could remember that, we'd all be happier and less stressed!

My heart is singing for joy this morning. A miracle has happened! The light of understanding has shown upon my little pupil's mind, and behold, all things are changed.

Anne Sullivan

Model the Skills You Teach

It is truly beyond comprehension how one individual, a teacher, Anne Sullivan, was able to release the extraordinary potentials locked inside of a little girl who could not see, speak, or hear: Helen Keller. How does one even begin? What incredible patience must one possess? The answer, for Anne Sullivan, was to begin at the very beginning, resolved to uncover the spirit, the intelligence, the profound thoughts and feelings, the talents, the gifts, and the beauty that embodied one of the most amazing women in history. And to think that Anne Sullivan accomplished all of this without lecturing, and without worksheets! Anne Sullivan "modeled" every skill she taught, and then Helen practiced and practiced with her teacher's guidance until she was ready to attempt the skill on her own. Fortunately, very few of us will ever teach a student with as many challenges as those that faced Helen Keller, yet all of us should model every skill we teach. This is how students begin to understand a concept—by "seeing" what it looks like. Unfortunately, teachers often overlook modeling when teaching a new skill. They tell, students listen, and then they send them off on their own. Yet students have never actually *seen* what they're supposed to perform. A common example is as follows: A teacher is teaching the students to write a descriptive paragraph. The teacher conducts a review of paragraph writing, the teacher and students discuss some descriptive words, the teacher describes the process of writing a descriptive paragraph, and then the students are given a topic on which to write a descriptive paragraph. Notice that the teacher never actually *modeled* the process of writing a descriptive paragraph for the students. Students need to see what the process looks like and listen as the teacher thinks aloud and models the thought processes that go into writing the paragraph. Then, the teacher and students should write a class paragraph, thinking it through together. This way, when the students are to perform the task on their own, they will have a mental picture of the process, along with some guided practice under their belts. Imagine teaching someone to swim without ever showing them what swimming *looks like*. Imagine teaching someone to ride a bike without ever showing them what bike riding *looks like*. That would be ludicrous, yet we do it every day in the classroom! Teaching, in any form, requires modeling.

If I model as I teach, an understanding they will reach!
And then I'll guide them through it, and soon they'll be able to do it!

*Children learn as children play, so play
with your students every day!*

Make Learning Fun

While I was conducting a presentation on effective teaching for high school
and university teachers, a college profes-
sor volunteered the following: "When I walked into the training today and learned
of the activities that were going to be conducted, I almost walked out. I thought
it was going to be 'elementary.' However, after participating in the activities and
having fun doing so, I realized that if I could have fun, maybe my students could
have fun as opposed to just listening to my daily lectures. And maybe I'd even have
fun teaching!" In response, a high school teacher enthusiastically added, "I do what
are considered 'elementary' activities with my students every day, and they love it!"
When I asked what she meant by 'elementary' activities, she explained that she uses
lots of cooperative learning, learning games, hands-on activities, group discussion,
and very little lecture. "My students love to come to class, because they have fun
and they experience so much success." A very interesting discussion ensued where
we discussed the fact that students learn best when they are having fun. "So do
adults!" added one of the participants.

Too often I encounter teachers who think that teaching and learning should be
"serious business." Their demeanors are serious, their classrooms are serious places,
their students are bored out of their minds, and discipline problems are evident. Not
very conducive to inspiring students to achieve! **The fact is that we all learn best
when the learning environment is interesting, exciting, and inviting.** Some teachers are afraid to allow their students to have "fun" in their classrooms for fear of
losing control of discipline. This is a mistake, in that **"fun" and "chaos" are not syn-
onymous.** Chaos is a classroom management problem. If classroom management
is well established, there will be no chaos. The best teachers know that in the most
effective learning environments, classroom management is established, students are
actively involved in the learning, lessons and activities are both highly structured
and of high interest to students, and students are enjoying the learning process. Yes,
they are having fun! Remember that taking teaching seriously and treating teaching
as strictly serious business are two very different things. So lighten up, add excitement to your lessons, and watch your students' achievement increase. Your students
will enjoy their learning, you will enjoy your teaching, and you will all have fun.

Don't look so serious when you're teaching, please don't!
If you don't have fun, then the students won't,
So take every lesson and teach it with zest
And you'll get from your students their very best!

I hear and I forget. I see and I remember. I do and I understand.

Chinese Proverb

Encourage Active Student Participation

Imagine that you are a student in a classroom where every day is the same. You walk into class, you open your textbook, the teacher lectures, and you take notes. You read a chapter, answer the questions at the end of the chapter, and complete worksheets. You define twenty vocabulary words, all of which must be memorized, along with your notes, for Friday's test. The teacher does the talking, and you do the sitting. You are expected to pay attention, be interested, keep quiet, and master your lessons. Imagine going through this every day for an entire school year! Where is the *teaching* in what I have just described? How much "sitting still" can any student endure? Where's the "doing" on the part of the students? Where are students actually solving problems or thinking critically? When has this type of teaching ever increased ANY student's achievement???

Now consider that you are a student in a classroom where no two days are alike. You have been studying the Civil War. The class has conducted research followed by discussions where students have interacted with the research and voiced opinions. Today, you are assigned to groups. Each group will be writing its thoughts on the war from different viewpoints: a Confederate soldier, a Union soldier, a slave owner, a slave, and the mother of a soldier. In completing your assignment, you will be using your own research. The teacher will interact with each group. Then, each group will present to the class. Discussions will follow each presentation. Can you see the difference between this lesson and the previous one? Did you recognize the teaching here, the active student participation, the interest level, the meaningful learning, and the lack of boredom? In which class would you prefer to be a student???

To rephrase the Chinese proverb above, "What I hear in the classroom goes in one ear and out the other, what I see in the classroom I tend to remember seeing, but what I actually have to do, I learn, and the learning sticks because I understand." Have your students DO as opposed to having them ENDURE!

What Has the Student Actually Learned?

*"Just take good notes and memorize the answers
    and learn each vocabulary word."*
*In far too many classrooms, this is far too often
    heard.*
*And if the notes are memorized to be spit back on
    Friday's test,*
*The student receives a passing grade and his
    parents are less distressed.*
*But what has the student actually learned? Does he
    even know?*
*He would if we got him to think and solve problems
    —and then what he's learned he can SHOW!*

                      A.L.B.

Challenge Students to Think Critically

A young boy I met at a friend's house enthusiastically told me that his favorite subject was math. He went on to tell me that he knew all of his multiplication facts very well. I obliged him by quizzing him. Sure enough, he knew the answers. When I asked him what was 4 x 4, he readily answered, "16." Then I asked, "What does that mean?" Again, he answered "16." I realized that the student had no concept of what multiplication actually meant. So the teacher in me broke into a quick lesson. After I explained the concept behind multiplication, he said, "Oh! Is that what that means? Do you mean that if I have four groups of people with four people in each group, that's the same as saying 4 x 4 = 16? I never knew that!" He immediately grabbed a deck of cards and started arranging them into groups and coming up with his own multiplication facts. I then had to sit with him for the next two hours and share in his enthusiasm, ignoring the group of adults with whom I had previously been visiting. The light bulb had gone on in a child's mind, and there was no turning it off! Beautiful!

The point I'm trying to make is that **we, as teachers, often assume too much. Just because a student knows an answer or can memorize a given piece of information, we assume that he understands.** This is often not the case. Knowing informational facts and being able to apply that information by thinking critically and using the information to solve problems are two different things.

I can remember the day that I figured out why we spent so much time in school diagramming sentences. I was always fairly adept at the skill, but I never really understood its purpose. Then one day, the light bulb went on, and I realized what the skill was all about. I couldn't believe I had *missed* that somewhere along the line. I now had a newfound understanding of the English language!

Critical thinking involves problem solving, which fosters a true understanding of a concept. Think about this. How many times, in your adult life, have you had to regurgitate the important battles of World War II? You *learned* them in your schooling, but unless you are a history buff, you probably don't remember them, nor do you need to in order to get along in life! What was important was to understand the reasons behind World War II: how and why it began, how and why we, as a nation, became involved, how people's lives were affected because of it, and how life as we know it today is influenced by the history that preceded it.

As a *fun* experiment, I took a group of 32 ninth graders and asked them to identify pronouns in a given set of sentences. With three exceptions, they were all able to complete the task successfully and accurately. Then I asked, "Now why do we have pronouns in our language, and how would life be different without them?" I received blank stares. Nothing. No answers. Then I had all of them attempt to tell me something about themselves without using pronouns. (You may want to attempt it yourself before you read on.) Within a minute, the students suddenly saw how awkward and cumbersome the language would be without the use of pronouns. It made sense! Then I took the three students who had had a little trouble with pronouns, provided quick remediation, and the light bulbs went on for them, too!

We need to make a special effort in our teaching to stop doling out facts and start encouraging students to think critically. Once they understand a concept, the facts become meaningful. This is the kind of thinking that arouses student interest, encourages them to delve deeply into concepts, and urges them to remain in a continual state of questioning.

I may be smarter than you or I know
So challenge me to think, and we'll both know if that's so!

How much sense would it make to take a written exam in swimming in order to determine whether you are a good swimmer???

Use Authentic Means of Assessment

There is much debate in education and lots of controversy over the best means of assessing student work. Without any research and without any controversy, I will put the whole idea of authentic assessment into perspective for you. The word *authentic* means *real* or *valid*. **So, authentic assessment is a valid way of measuring whether your students have attained a particular skill.** In the question above, even the slightest bit of common sense reveals that assessing the skill of swimming by using a written test is ludicrous. Authentic assessment of this skill would require that the student actually swim. So it is with any skill that we teach. In order to determine a student's knowledge of particular vocabulary, regurgitating a memorized definition tells us nothing. The student must actually be able to *use* the vocabulary words. **A written test on the scientific method is not valid if the student is only required to list the steps in the scientific method. He must be able to apply the method to a given experiment.** Giving a set of questions based on a reading story that has been discussed all week in class is really a test in memory as opposed to a test in reading comprehension. In order to know if students can truly comprehend what they read, they must be tested with unfamiliar text.

If you want to know if a person can cook, then have the person cook something. Apply that same logic in your classroom! In assessing student work, decide what it is that you want to assess, and then assess it in a way that is "real" and "valid." It's really that simple!

With a written test on swimming, the chances are less than slim
That you will be able to determine if I am able to swim.
Allow me to swim around every day in all of the content you teach,
And chances are looking better and better that understanding I'll reach!

Same Old Same Old

Same old same old, same thing every day;
My brain just disconnects, for when it's
* bored it does not play.*
But change the routine up a bit and my
* brain will scream, "Hooray!"*
Engage me and surprise me and I will
* not drift away.*

                              A.L.B.

Vary Your Teaching Strategies

Wow! Gotcha! What, how, why? You caught me by surprise. Oh my!

It is human nature to be intrigued by "the element of surprise." **Students respond favorably to teachers who keep them intrigued, wondering what exciting thing will happen next.** Let's be clear, however, that I am referring to teaching strategies and not to classroom management strategies. Regarding routines and procedures in the classroom—how to enter the room, when to focus attention on the teacher, how to pass in papers, how to ask for permission to speak, what to do when there is a fire drill, etc.—there is no room for the *element of surprise!* These procedures should remain consistent, so as not to become confusing or chaotic. But regarding teaching strategies, spice it up. As the saying goes, "Variety is the spice of life." Successful teachers know this, and they use every opportunity to capitalize on this with their students.

We can all recall sitting in classrooms where the only variety that we noticed was the change of the date on the calendar every day. It was the same old same old, day in and day out. We walked into class, we opened our textbooks, the teacher lectured, we took notes, and you know the rest of the routine. When I spoke to a middle school student about his favorite teacher, he said, "What's really great about Mr. Carter's class is that we never know what to expect. Some days we walk into class and he's dressed as the character we'll be discussing. Other days, he's hurrying us into the room saying, 'You won't believe what I have in store for you today.' The man is so full of energy that we all seem to 'catch' it. He keeps us moving all the time. Some days he wears us out. It's always something different—not that old boring lecture stuff that we get from some of our other teachers. All the kids love him, and even the tough kids behave in Mr. Carter's class."

I think you'll agree that this student's words say a lot. However, the icing on the cake was when a fifth-grade student described her "favorite" teacher and the importance of variety in teaching. She said, with a giant smile on her face, "Ms. Barton is like chicken, but the good kind." "What do you mean?" I asked. "Well,

I'll tell you what the bad kind is first. With some teachers, going to their class is like eating plain old chicken, cooked the same way, every single day. Even if you like it at first, you get tired of eating chicken cooked the same way all the time. But in Ms. Barton's class, some days it's fried chicken, some days it's barbecued chicken, some days it's chicken soup, some days it's baked chicken, and some days it's chicken nuggets, but it's always cooked really well—and all the kids like it, so we eat a lot of it, and we never get tired of it because it always changes." "Wow!" I thought. "From the mouths of babes."

Vary your teaching strategies. Move quickly from exciting explanations to inviting discussions to interesting hands-on learning activities to class projects to student demonstrations of skills, and so on. Change your routine so that your lessons do not always look the same. Do you know how many ways there are to prepare chicken?

What's Best for My Students

Do I do what's best for my students or
*   what's easiest for me?*
For it's easier, yes, to sit at my desk and
*   let each be his own busy bee,*
But "busy work" becomes "dizzy work"
*   and the students soon will resent it,*
And as anyone knows, their frustration
*   grows, and soon they will all need to*
*   vent it.*
Yes, teaching takes work, and you simply can't shirk
What's best for what's unproblematic
Because if you do, what's easiest for you will soon lead to all things erratic.
So choose what's best for your students, and never what's easiest for you,
For nothing worthwhile, such as reaching a child, will ever be easy to do!

A.L.B., *101 Poems for Teachers*

Do What's Best, Not What's Easiest

It's not always easy to be positive, but being positive <u>is</u> best for your students. It would be easier to dole out *busy work,* but that's <u>not</u> what's best for your students. It is far easier to let the textbook tell you exactly what to teach as opposed to simply using the textbook as one of several references, but letting the textbook make your decisions is <u>not</u> what's best for your students. An objective test consisting only of multiple choice and true-false items is far easier for a teacher to grade than a more authentic form of assessment, but doing what's easy is not what's best for your students. Planning lessons that engage students continually is time consuming, but it <u>is</u> what's best for your students. The old *lecture, read the chapter, answer the questions at the end of the chapter* method of teaching is easy, again, for the teacher, but it's <u>not</u> what's best for your students. Teaching all students as if they were on the same level is far easier than teaching students at their individual levels, but it's <u>not</u> what's best for students. Being professional at all costs is not always easy, but it <u>is</u> what's best for your students.

What's best and what's easiest often conflict, but do what is best and contradict what's easy and breezy and makes you contrite. Do what you know in your heart is right!

Professionalism:
Attitudes and Behaviors
of Effective Teachers

I Bleed Professionalism

I bleed professionalism, yet I don't need medical attention.
The blood is not the red kind, but the kind of another dimension—
A dimension where I am a role model, and my blood spills onto each student.
From me, I hope they will learn to be sensible, practical, prudent,
For everything I do and say is under their scrutiny
Because everything I do and say influences who they will be.
My coworkers watch me also—I'm under a microscope.
They wait to see just how I'll react in a tough situation and cope.
So I'm careful about my words, my dress, and the look upon my face.
One's professionalism or lack of it can make or break a place!

A.L.B., *Seven Simple Secrets*

Want to know who the best teachers in the school are? ASK THE STUDENTS!

Maintain a Positive Reputation

Every teacher, in every classroom, on every school campus has a *reputation*. If you have taught more than one week, you have a reputation. Students quickly identify the caring teachers, the screamers, the ones who give the most homework, the ones who hold the record for office referrals, etc. Consider the fact that most parents never see their children's teachers teach. But almost all parents have an opinion of their children's teachers. For the most part, parents judge the reputations of teachers based on what their children tell them. And teachers know the reputations of their counterparts also. **You do not have to observe a teacher in the classroom to make a fairly accurate determination of that teacher's character and effectiveness in the classroom.** You can watch teachers take their classes to lunch and tell whether management is in place. You can watch teachers interact with children on the school grounds and know what kind of rapport they do or don't share. You can walk down the hallways and know who's teaching. And you can listen to their conversations with others and learn a lot about their attitudes, their professionalism, and their overall effectiveness. Also, whether you want to or not, you will overhear students talking about their teachers. No teacher wants to have a negative reputation, yet many do. So how do you avoid becoming one of the teachers with a negative reputation? **The best way to steer clear of a negative reputation is not to establish one in the first place** because once you have one, it's extremely difficult to change it. If you simply teach from your heart, treat your students with dignity, carry yourself as a professional, and approach each day with dedication and enthusiasm, you will be able to enjoy and DESERVE your positive reputation!

Resist any temptation that could spark a negative connotation, and instead commit to your vocation and earn a positive reputation.

The Cookie Thief

A woman was waiting at an airport one
* night,*
With several long hours before her flight.
She hunted for a book in the airport shop,
Bought a bag of cookies and found a place to
* drop.*
She was engrossed in her book, but happened
* to see,*
That the man beside her, as bold as could be,
Grabbed a cookie or two from the bag
* between,*
Which she tried to ignore to avoid a scene.
She read, munched cookies, and watched the clock
As the gutsy "cookie thief" diminished her stock
She was getting more irritated as the minutes ticked by
Thinking, "If I weren't so nice, I'd blacken his eye!"
With each cookie she took, he took one too.
When only one was left, she wondered what he'd do.
With a smile on his face and a nervous laugh,
He took the last cookie and broke it in half.
He offered her half, as he ate the other.
She snatched it from him and thought, "Oh, brother!
This guy has some nerve and he's also rude.
Why, he didn't even show any gratitude!"
She had never known when she had been so galled,
And sighed with relief when her flight was called.
She gathered her belongings and headed for the gate
Refusing to look back at that "thieving ingrate."
She boarded the plane and sank in her seat,
Then sought her book which was almost complete.
As she reached in her baggage, she gasped with surprise.
There was her bag of cookies in front of her eyes!
"If mine are here," she moaned with despair,
"Then the others were his and he tried to share!"
Too late to apologize, she realized with grief,
That she was the rude one, the ingrate, the thief!

Valerie Cox

Tip 47

Do Not Fall Prey to Feeling Victimized

As you read the poem "The Cookie Thief," you soon realize that the woman, who seems a victim at first, is only a victim in her mind. Her perception of the situation is leading her to feel victimized. She believes he is stealing from her and she is insulted and incensed, until she later realizes that the opposite is true and that SHE is actually the "cookie thief." How embarrassing!

Likewise, teachers are not victims of their jobs! We all picked our jobs. We proudly presented our credentials and interviewed for jobs that were offered to us. We then signed our names on the dotted lines of our contracts. We chose this profession. At any time, we are free to choose another. So how can we be victims of something we have chosen and continue to choose??? We can't be! Yet often you will hear conversations that sound something like this: "Can you believe what they're asking us to do? What do they think we are—superhuman?" And here's another common scenario: "If I could get rid of five students in my class, my life would be so wonderful. I think they gave me those students on purpose. And I'm sorry, but it's impossible to teach when you've got students acting like animals in your classroom. And don't bother sending them to the office because nothing will be done. They just send them right back." And one more: "It must be wonderful to sit in an ivory tower barking out orders while we're killing ourselves in our classrooms. And to think that administrators get paid more than we do! What a joke, and what a waste of money!"

Do not let yourself fall prey to feeling victimized! It's a dangerous road that leads to frustration, anger, self-righteousness, and all that is negative and harmful, not only to you, but also to the children whose lives you continue to influence daily.

We are not victims, cut and bleeding, desperately needing sutures.
Rather, we have chosen to have our hands hold students' futures.

FACT: Circumstances don't make the teacher. Circumstances reveal the teacher.

Choose Your Reactions

We often have very <u>little</u> control over our circumstances, but we have very <u>much</u> control over how we choose to react to those circumstances. In the classroom, students will work diligently at determining who you are as a person and a teacher. They are masters at reading adults. They are masters at pushing adults' buttons. They will try to make you stop, stare at the ceiling, and lose your patience. They will try to see if they can make you clench your teeth as you speak in an angry tone. They will even try to see how far they can make the vein stick out on the side of your neck! If you allow them to control you, you will belong to them as opposed to having them belong to you. Don't give in. Never forget that YOU choose your reactions in any situation.

I know a teacher who is always assigned the "problem" students. She teaches the ones no one else wants to teach, due to their prior histories of misbehavior. But this teacher knows how to choose her reactions very carefully. Each year, she welcomes the opportunity to teach the "un-teachables." She treats them with dignity, patience, and respect. She has high expectations for all. Oh yes, they "try" her at first. It happens every year. But the fact that she never gives them the reactions they're seeking soon neutralizes them. When they realize that she will not lose her temper, that she will not stop believing in them, and that she will do anything to make them successful, they stop trying to provoke negative responses from her. It works every year, as her record has shown. And her influence on her students is nothing short of profound.

Remember, your circumstances will never <u>determine</u> who you are, but rather your reactions to circumstances will <u>reveal</u> who you are to students, parents, and coworkers. Choose your reactions!

When you get angry, don't let it show, 'cause if you do, then they will know, and once they know, that's it, you're through; you belong to them, not them to you!

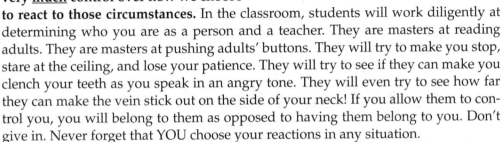

Mrs. WarnYa

On every single faculty, there lives a Mrs.
*   WarnYa*
Like a very heavy necklace, if you let her, she'll
*   adorn ya*
She warns of all the troubled kids and bad
*   administration*
She'll show you, if you'll listen, how to seek
*   retaliation*
With bitterness, her nectar, and doom, her
*   jubilation*
She never seems to realize that her actual
*   revelation*
Is admitting she's a gossip, admitting she's a
*   fake*
Befriending Mrs. WarnYa is always a mistake!

    A.L.B., *101 Poems for Teachers*

Don't Let Negative Coworkers Affect You

Tip 49

FACT: If there are more than three people on your school's faculty, then chances are good that there's a negative faction! This is not to suggest that the majority of teachers are negative individuals. They're not. But one negative individual can have a tremendous negative influence on other coworkers. To date, I have yet to find a faculty that has been spared of a Mrs. WarnYa.

As teachers, we all stand at a fork in the road where we are faced with a very important decision. We can choose to go "left"—fitting in and falling prey—or we can choose to go "right"—doing what's best for students, the only way! The fact is that you will not be alone on either path you choose. One way, however, is more difficult. It takes more guts. Which is that? The "right" way. Let's look at what you'll get on each path.

If you go "right" and do what's best for students, there are both pros and cons:

Pros: *Your classroom will be an exciting place, student achievement will rise, student self-esteem will rise, you will be highly respected by respectable educators, and your contribution to society will be immeasurable.*

Cons: *You will work hard, and you will run the risk of being scrutinized by the people who chose to go "left."*

Final destination: *You will be a happy, successful, hard-working, contributing, truly effective, highly qualified, and highly respected teacher who touches lives and makes a difference.*

If you go "left" and choose to fit in and fall prey, there are also pros and cons:

Pros: *All the negative people will like you, you will be allowed to gripe all you want, and your workload will be lightened by the overuse of worksheets, busy* *work, and time-fillers. Also, you will experience the bliss of denial by simply blaming society, parents, administration, and students, conveniently forgetting that you have total control, with very few exceptions, over what goes on in your classroom.*

Cons*: You will very likely struggle with management and discipline, but it will at least give you something more to gripe about. You will know all the latest gossip, your cynical attitude will breed resentment in students, respectable educators will have no respect for you, and last, but definitely not least, you may figure out one day that you've taken the wrong road, and you'll be sorry.*

Final destination*: You will find yourself a burned out, cynical, bitter individual who missed out on all the rewards of teaching and touching lives.*

The choice seems obvious, but remember that the main difference between truly effective and truly ineffective teachers lies in the choices they have made along the way. Make the "right" choice!

Please, Teacher

Please, teacher, treat my child as if he were your own.
For if you do, I'm more likely to
Answer when you phone,
More likely to work beside you, less likely to cause you woe.
I've sent you the best that I have to offer, and to me, he's great. Don't you know?

A.L.B.

Tip 50

Learn to Work Cooperatively with Parents

One of the biggest fears of new teachers is dealing with parents—namely the angry ones. And, **if a new teacher does not know a few simple tricks for working cooperatively with parents, parent conferences can be unsuccessful and downright frightening experiences.** So read on if you would like to learn ways to work cooperatively with parents—even the angry ones.

As I walked down the hall of a high school, I met up with a new teacher who was in tears. I asked what was wrong, and she answered, "I'm on my way to call a parent who's really upset with me, and I don't know how to defend myself against her." "Why is she upset with you?" I asked. "Well, we sent out letters to invite parents to come in for private conferences. This parent claims she never got the letter, but I know I mailed all of them." "Okay," I said. "I'm going to walk you through this. First of all, let's capitalize on the very positive fact that this parent cares enough about her child's education to want to come to a conference." "I never thought about it that way," said the new teacher. I then told her exactly what to say during the phone conversation. Here are the instructions I gave her.

- Begin by saying, "I understand that you're very upset about not receiving a letter regarding the parent conferences. And I just want you to know that I was very impressed with the fact that you cared enough about your son to want to come to school and meet with his teacher. That says a lot about you as a parent."

- Then say, "I'm so sorry that you didn't receive the letter. But I'm anxious to meet with you, and I'm willing to do my best to accommodate your schedule."

- Next, ask, "What would be a convenient time for us to meet?"

Notice that nothing in the above conversation was in any way defensive. That's important, because when parents are angry, teachers often make the mistake of engaging in the struggle and arguing with them. What they should really do is allow the parent to express his/her concerns, remaining calm and professional throughout. You see, **when a person is angry, the anger can only last so long, unless, of course, the other party is fueling it.** If the other party remains calm and does not become defensive, the angry parent will soon run out of steam. That's the opportunity to begin solving the problem.

Anyway, the new teacher went into the office to use the phone and I waited out in the hall. About five minutes later, she walked out of the office beaming. She said to me, "We're best friends now! She and I really hit it off after I complimented her on her genuine concern for her son. We're meeting tomorrow."

Yes, it really can be that simple. Approach all parents with the assumption that they truly do want what's best for their children, and work cooperatively and professionally with them in helping to achieve a common goal. Listen to them when they are upset, let them blow off steam if necessary, and then establish the fact that you're anxious to work cooperatively with them to solve the problem. Also, try to ensure that your comments about a child include the child's strengths. Make it a practice to establish positive communication with parents up front, and then when the occasional negative situation occurs, they will be much more willing to work cooperatively with you in solving the problem. A parent is much more likely to support you when he believes that you are genuinely interested in his child. And even if a parent walks out of a conference disagreeing with you, make sure that he or she walks out knowing that you acted professionally and did not lose your cool. You might not be able to control all of an angry parent's reactions, but you can most certainly control your own reactions in every such situation.

Remember that working cooperatively with a parent can save you stress and woe,
You both want the same thing—what's best for his child—so be a teammate, not a foe.

Who's to Blame?

The college professor said, "Such rawness in a student is a shame. Lack of preparation in high school is to blame."

Said the high school teacher, "Good heavens, that boy's a fool. The fault, of course, is with the middle school."

The middle school teacher said, "From stupidity may I be spared. They sent him in so unprepared."

The primary teacher huffed, "Kindergarten blockheads all. They call that preparation? Why, it's worse than none at all."

The kindergarten teacher said, "Such lack of training never did I see. What kind of woman must that mother be?"

The mother said, "Poor helpless child. He's not to blame. His father's people were all the same."

Said the father at the end of the line, "I doubt the rascal's even mine."

Anonymous

Steer Clear of the Blame Game

Any teacher, any parent, and any child can relate to "Who's to Blame." Why? Because we've all been guilty of it. But the simple fact is that playing the blame game does us no good. It does not move us forward, it does not help children, it does not improve teaching, and it wastes our valuable time and energy. There's only one piece of advice I can give you regarding the blame game: DON'T PARTICIPATE!

Every year, we receive a certain group of students. We do not get to "pick" them. We do not get to pick their parents. We do not have any say in their educational experiences prior to teaching them. We do, however, get to take them as they are and help them to grow from there. If we are committed to doing that, then we have no time for blaming. We have only time, and not nearly enough of it, to teach every one of them, to share our gifts, to recognize theirs, and to help them become what they are capable of becoming.

The blame game is a lame game! If you play, then dearly you'll pay!

She Cheered for Me

There must be some type of crazy
*   malfunction,*
For my teacher was at my after-
*   school function.*
I thought my teacher lived in her
*   classroom at school.*
Did they let her out? 'Cause it's
*   extremely cool*
That my teacher cared enough to
*   come to the game.*
She cheered for me, so, for her I'll
*   do the same!*

                    A.L.B.

Participate in After-School Functions

We all have lives of our own outside of our classrooms. If you're a new teacher, then you're the exception. (Just kidding—but I know it feels like you don't have a life outside of school right now!) Whenever possible, however, it is important to participate in after-school functions. I'll share a personal experience here. When I was in third grade, my sisters, a couple of friends, and I invited my third-grade teacher, Mrs. Robichaux, to a talent show that we were planning. Little did we dream that she would actually attend. In fact, we were so convinced that she wouldn't come that we never got around to planning the talent show. But guess what? She showed up! We went into a panic, because we had nothing planned. We quickly hung a sheet on the clothesline—our curtain—seated Mrs. Robichaux in a chair, and huddled behind the curtain to come up with something, anything! Thank goodness that my younger sister, Andrée, loved to perform. We kept sending her out to entertain Mrs. Robichaux. She first sang, "Leaving on a Jet Plane." Mrs. Robichaux clapped enthusiastically, and Andrée returned to us behind the curtain. We then sent her out to exhibit her gymnastic abilities. The poor little thing, only 6 years old at the time, was exhausted. But each time we sent her out, Mrs. Robichaux acted as though it was the most amazing talent she had ever witnessed. Then we all came out, took a bow, and Mrs. Robichaux left. In retrospect, I'm sure that Mrs. Robichaux knew, after the first act, that we had nothing prepared. But she never let on. She never even commented on the fact that the only participant in the talent show was my little sister. The following day, she thanked us for inviting her and said how much she had enjoyed herself. And we realized how much Mrs. Robichaux cared. She gave of her own time, after school hours, to watch a six-year-old turn cartwheels across the yard. Is that dedication or what?

You see, participation in after-school functions sends a message to students and to parents that you care. No, our mother was not happy with us when she learned of what we had put poor Mrs. Robichaux through. However, she was definitely impressed with the fact that Mrs. Robichaux had not only endured, but pretended to enjoy our "talent" show. Parents who believe that you care about their children will be much more likely to support you and work cooperatively with you. Students who believe that you care about them will work harder, will behave better, and will even "turn cartwheels" for you! As the saying goes, "Students won't care how much you know until they know how much you care."

P. S. Andrée went on to receive a Master's Degree in the Performing Arts. We think that Mrs. Robichaux's unbridled enthusiasm and encouragement had something to do with it!

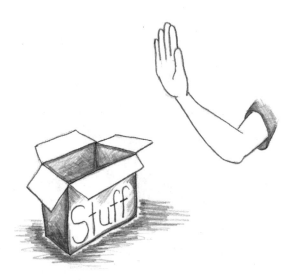

Stuff, stuff, they gave her more stuff,
But no matter how much they gave her, it was never enough
For the great teachers don't need stuff to make them great
And all the stuff in the world won't improve a poor teacher's fate!

Resist the Temptation for More "Stuff"

Researchers tell us that the effects of an ineffective teacher can be seen in student test scores years down the road. To some, that research seems amazing. Isn't it funny, however, that we do not need research to tell us that the effects of an ineffective surgeon can be seen in patient x-rays years down the road? That's just common sense! Question: If patients are dying on a particular surgeon's operating table, do we simply buy the surgeon a new scalpel, a new video series, or, better yet, spruce up the operating room? Can you see where I'm going with this? **Why is it that when students are not achieving in our classrooms, we tend to buy more "stuff," implement more programs, or, better yet, spruce up the physical surroundings???** To prove this point, put yourself in the position of a parent who has a choice between two schools for your child. Would you choose a school with little resources, few programs, but all effective teachers or would you choose a school with lots of money, every program imaginable, but all ineffective teachers? As a new teacher, in which of the above two schools would you choose to teach? As an administrator, in which school would you want to work? The fact is that I have yet to meet a parent, a teacher, or an administrator who would opt for the school with ineffective teachers. As teachers, we don't need more "stuff." What we need are good models, supportive surroundings, and a desire to continue to improve our teaching skills. I'm not against programs, but just remember, no amount of stuff will make us better teachers. And even the most effective of educational programs will fall flat in the hands of an ineffective teacher. **Just as the scalpel is only as good as the surgeon, a teaching tool is only as good as the teacher using it.**

Ineffective teachers focus on hoarding "stuff" to cure their ills.
Effective teachers focus on honing their skills!

By swallowing evil words unsaid,
no one has ever yet harmed his stomach.
Winston Churchill

Avoid Lounge Gossip

Have you been warned yet to stay away from the teachers' lounge? Have you heard that that's where the gossips gather? Whether they gather in the lounge or elsewhere, they are usually present in every school. It's sad, because most teachers are genuinely good people. I've always believed that any teacher gossiping about students does not know this very important fact: **Gossip serves one purpose: it HARMS!**

I've always thought that a wonderful benefit for both teachers and students is the fact that we have the advantage of being able to start over every year. Imagine if you, as a teacher, would continue to be evaluated by your administrator based on previous mistakes you have made in your teaching or in your life, for that matter. Many of us would be doomed before we even began a new year. But sadly, many students are "doomed" each year because of the careless, harmful words spoken about them between teachers. If you are a teacher, you will encounter others, somewhere along the way, who will try to engage with you in empty, meaningless gossip. Do not participate. Not only is it unprofessional, but it symbolizes the antithesis of what we truly stand for: serving and helping others. If you can't say something nice about someone, don't say anything.

And please don't stay away from the lounge. You need and deserve an occasional break! I encourage you to go into the lounge every chance you get and be the most positive person there. Speak only well of students and encourage all of the positive teachers to join you in the lounge. Soon, the negative people will be so uncomfortable that they'll leave, and the lounge will become a positive, gossip-free zone!

The sour grapes will soon fall from the vine,
And the sweetest grapes will make the finest wine!
Cheers!

Tip 54

There's only ONE reason to become a teacher
To teach every child—to reach him and reach her
And to make all decisions based on what is best
for each
So that you can proudly proclaim, "I touch the
world—I teach!"

Remind Yourself Why You Chose to Become a Teacher

Okay, so we all entered the profession of teaching for the same reason: the money! (Ha!) Seriously, I believe that, as teachers, we all share a common calling and a common purpose. In my training sessions with teachers, I often begin by having them state why they entered the profession. It is always inspirational to hear the same thing, yet stated in unique ways by each teacher. The prevailing theme? "I wanted to make a difference, to touch lives." And it never fails. Following the training session, someone always comes to me and says, "Thanks for helping me to remember why I became a teacher. I had almost forgotten."

In the everyday mayhem of our lives, we often get "caught up" in the negatives. It can happen in our personal lives and in our professional lives. **In teaching, it is sometimes all too easy to lose sight of our main focus, our students.** I once had a meeting with a teacher who just needed to "vent." The conversation went like this: "I can't understand why we've adopted yet another new program. The pendulum just keeps swinging back and forth. I'm up to my ears in paperwork, and I've just been asked to chair yet another committee. The whole educational system seems to be going down like a sinking ship. When are we going to get a break? Why don't they just leave us alone?" After listening to her express her frustrations, I said, "Tell me what made you choose this profession." The teacher went on to share a touching story about a teacher who had influenced her life in so many ways. She said, "Realizing what a difference she made with me, one student of many, I decided that that's what I wanted to do—make a difference in the lives of children, just as my teacher had done for me." I didn't have to say another word. The teacher smiled warmly and said, "Thanks for reminding me of that. I guess I was losing sight of the only thing that really matters in this profession—making a difference."

Yes, teaching is stressful and at times overwhelming. **When you feel like you're at the end of your rope, remind yourself that YOU are a rope—a lifeline for the students that you teach.**

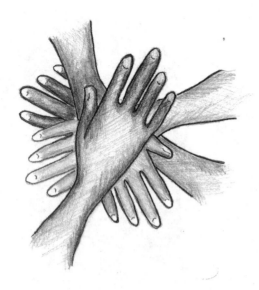

Administrators, mentor teachers,
students, parents, police, and preachers
Most of these people will help with a task
and be honored to do so, if only you'll ASK!

Enlist the Support
of Others

Since the real world happens outside of the classroom, it's often good to bring it INTO the classroom! As a teacher said to me recently, "I'm not a one-man show. I enlist the support of anyone who can provide assistance in helping my students to learn." This was a high school teacher who had his students help him in decorating the room, gathering materials for activities, and just about anything else with which he needed help. He often had community members serving as guest speakers in his classroom. A group of volunteer parents were regularly in his classroom assisting with a multitude of tasks. And he even had other teachers coming in to demonstrate techniques for the benefit of both him and his students. He was a mentor to a new teacher, and he claimed that he got more new and innovative ideas from the new teacher than from any other member on the staff. "I believe in teamwork," he said. "When you get everyone involved, not only does it keep your classroom interesting, but it lets parents feel like active participants in their children's education. It also allows for community involvement, which is beneficial to all." His science project demonstrations were always the *hit* of the year, and he invited everyone to attend. "Anyone is welcomed in our classroom. But I'm warning you, if you walk in, we'll put you to work."

Not only was this teacher willing to enlist the support of others in the education of his students, but the students also went into the community to volunteer their time in assisting others. "It's a reciprocal kind of thing," he said. "We accept assistance from others, and we give something back. I think the most surprising thing to many is that so many people—colleagues, administrators, parents, community members, etc.—are so willing to help. All you have to do is ask!"

Seize every opportunity to involve the community!

When we do the best we can, we never know what miracle is wrought in our life, or in the life of another.
Helen Keller

Be the Best You Can Be

There is little in life that gives us more satisfaction than knowing that we have done something and given it our best. Teaching gives us that opportunity every day. **No teacher is perfect.** All teachers make mistakes. (Hey, new teachers, we veterans still haven't finished learning to teach, so we still make lots of mistakes. But the best teachers try not to make the same mistakes twice.) Regardless of the fact that we do make mistakes, teachers who give their best every day are the ones who touch lives. **In teaching, even the most difficult days can be successful ones when we are resolved to give it our all.** In fact, the most difficult days are often the most rewarding ones—those days when we are truly put to the test. There will be days when you are not feeling well, either emotionally or physically, but if you choose to come to school, you must be at your best. There will be days when students try your patience because they do not understand what you're trying to teach. Again, try a new way of explaining it and do not give in to frustration. Do not give up, and do not give in. Rather, give it all you've got—and then some.

It is only in giving our best that we can possibly expect to bring out the best in our students. And in doing our best, we never know "what miracle is wrought…in the life of another." So be the best teacher you can be, and your rewards will come to you in the form of young hearts, young lives forever changed because of your influence.

Which Way?

I stood at a fork in the road
And didn't know which way to go
But since I had no destination in mind
If I got there, I'd never know!

A.L.B.

Set Goals for Your Own Improvement

FACT: Written goals are far more likely to be accomplished than mental goals. Most people have goals, lots of them. But many people never accomplish them. Consider New Year's resolutions. "I'm going to get skinny." "I'm going to save more money." "I'm going to get rid of the clutter in my house." "I'm going to be a nicer person." Notice how vague these goals are. There's no real plan of action, so they usually aren't accomplished. It would be far more "doable" to say, "I'm going to walk 20 minutes a day, three days a week." "I'm going to increase my monthly contributions to my savings by 5%." "I'm going to have a garage sale to get rid of things around the house that I don't need." "I'm going to make a special effort to do something nice for someone, just one thing, every day." And then you write them down and keep them in a place where you will see them daily. Goals are accomplished one step at a time. And written goals are much more likely to be accomplished than non-written ones!

In the classroom, you might say, "I'm going to learn to implement cooperative learning this year." "I'm going to devise a new classroom management plan and implement it consistently." "I'm going to write student-oriented activities into my lesson plans daily."

Whatever your goals, write them and post them. Take one step toward your goals every day, and you're sure to arrive there. Don't just stand at the fork in the road scratching your head. Have the end in mind first, map out your plan, and drive toward your destination without taking any detours.

Even one step a day will ensure that you move
Toward accomplishing your goal—which will help you improve
Because each time a teacher's teaching improves, student success improves too
So don't just wish, but reach a goal! It will help your students and YOU!

As the old saying goes: Blessed are the flexible, for they shall not be bent out of shape!

Be Flexible

Any teacher will tell you that in teaching there are both predictabilities and un-predictabilities. Here are some of the un-predictabilities:

- ◆ Fire drills
- ◆ Unexpected intercom announcements
- ◆ Children getting sick
- ◆ Unexpected discipline challenges
- ◆ Unanticipated student questions
- ◆ Schedule changes
- ◆ Knocks at the classroom door
- ◆ Unannounced observations by administration
- ◆ Running out of time to teach a particular skill
- ◆ Overestimating the time it will take to teach a particular skill
- ◆ Policy changes
- ◆ Changes in teaching assignments, and so on and so on and so on…

The only real predictability in teaching is the fact that it is unpredictable. Get accustomed to it. Don't let yourself get bent out of shape by things over which you have no control. Be flexible. If you don't learn to bend, you're going to eventually break!

> *When an un-predictability causes you to shake,*
> *You have a choice to bend or break*
> *So choose to bend rather than break,*
> *And roll with the punches, for sanity's sake!*

Tip 60

Learn and Grow from Your Mistakes

In Tip 29, we discussed how to recover quickly when making mistakes. In Tip 100, we will discuss teaching students that mistakes are wonderful learning opportunities. In this tip, we will focus on learning and growing from our own mistakes—practicing what we preach to our students. Mistakes are everywhere. We all make them, and we make them often. They are always a means to learning and growing, if we allow them to be.

It was my first year of teaching. My students were eagerly awaiting the "trial run" for the science fair. I set a table in the front of the classroom, and my students began to display and explain their projects. One student's project involved helium. He was going to demonstrate, with an actual model, how a hot air balloon works. I sat anxiously in the back of the room waiting to see the magic. Just as he was about to light the match, one of the students looked at me and asked, "Don't you think we'd better go outside for this experiment, since it involves fire?" How could I have been so stupid? I quickly agreed, and we took the experiment outside. Sure enough, something went wrong with the experiment, and the balloon burst into flames. What a close call! My dear, sweet students never said a word, but I'm sure they knew how I was feeling: relieved and dimwitted. When we returned to the room, I thanked them for their excellent display of common sense, and I learned a very important lesson about thinking in advance and using common sense.

Every mistake provides a chance to learn and grow. You will make lots of them. Don't repeat them, though!

Too Many Questions

You say I ask too many questions
But you just don't seem to see
That I wonder about so many things
For which answers there surely must be
But once I know an answer
A new question grows in my mind
Because what I learn uncovers
New problems with answers to find
So be patient with my questioning
There still is so much I don't know
But I do know that learning more answers
Will certainly help me to grow.
                   A.L.B., 101 Poems for Teachers

Ask Lots of Questions

New teachers are often afraid to ask questions. Said a new teacher, "I have so many questions, but I don't know whom to ask. I'm afraid to look stupid, so I can't ask other teachers. They'll probably think I should know these things. Then my reputation will suffer. But I need answers!" Sadly, this is a very typical concern of new teachers. They're afraid to ask, for fear of appearing incompetent. This is what they do not yet know:

- Teaching is not an exact science, so all teachers should remain in a state of questioning.
- Teachers, in general, are more than willing to share their techniques, ideas, and philosophies.
- Asking questions does not make you look incompetent. Rather, it makes you look like a dedicated professional who wants to do what's best for students.
- True professionals will not sacrifice learning something new for fear of appearing ignorant. We are all ignorant when it comes to teaching. There's so much we don't yet know.

If you want to be an effective teacher, you can't afford NOT to ask questions. **Any teacher, regardless of years of experience, who does not question will stagnate.** So ask lots of questions. Just be prepared for the fact that every time you get one question answered, it will open a whole new world of possibilities, for which you'll have more questions, which will, of course, lead to more answers which will then awaken new questions which will require more answers.

Any questions???

Students judge you, partly, by your dress
When you don't look like a professional,
they respect you less...

Dress Like a Professional

If you walked through a crowded airport, you would instantly be able to spot pilots and flight attendants because they are professionally dressed in uniform. That is because when you step onto an airplane, you want to feel like you are in capable, competent hands. But wouldn't the pilot be just as capable and competent if he were dressed in tennis shoes and blue jeans? Yes, but the passengers would not view him that way. So the uniforms are intentional.

If you walked into a courtroom, could you spot the attorneys? Consider this: If you were accused of a crime that you did not commit, and on the day of your trial your attorney arrived in blue jeans and tennis shoes, you would immediately think, "I'm going to jail." Not because the attorney is less competent, but because the jurors, the ones who will determine your fate, would not take him seriously.

It has been proven, time and again, that **the way we dress often influences the way others perceive us**. So let's take this into a school. There they are—hundreds of anxious, perceptive, role-model-seeking students waiting to form perceptions of their teachers. And here come the teachers. How are they dressed? That depends. A sad fact is that you could not walk into most schools and immediately spot all of the teachers based on their professional attire. Some you would recognize, instantly, as teachers. Others would be dressed in blue jeans and tennis shoes. Does that make them less competent? No. But it does change the way their students perceive them, which affects their effectiveness!

Teaching is the noblest profession of all. So why don't all teachers dress the part? Does that mean that you should go out, on your meager salary, and buy expensive clothing? No. It does, however, mean that you should not dress like your students. If you're going to be on your feet all day, don't expect to wear high heels. Just look like a professional! Here's a question to ask yourself before you leave for work each day: "If a stranger were to meet me on the street, would he know that I am some type of professional on my way to work?" If your answer is yes, then you are dressed professionally. If not, then go back to your closet and change—quickly—before the students see you! **So take a good look at yourself. Does your attire leave something to be desired?**

Tip from Breaux, A. & Whitaker, T. (2006). *Seven Simple Secrets: What the BEST Teachers Know and Do!* Larchmont, NY: Eye On Education.

If I, as your teacher, am allowed to grade you
Then why not allow you to grade me, too?

Devise a "Teacher Report Card"

Want to know how you're REALLY doing as a teacher? Ask your students.

During my third year of teaching, I read, in a magazine for teachers, about the idea of a "teacher report card." I thought to myself, "My students receive report cards, yet they never get the opportunity to evaluate me, to tell me how *I'm* doing as their teacher. I loved the idea, though I must admit that it was a bit frightening, knowing that my students would be brutally honest with me. But who better to judge my effectiveness than my own students? They were my "clients." I was there to serve them. Why shouldn't they be allowed to provide me with feedback as to how I was doing? I implemented the idea immediately, and the students loved it. They were a little amazed at the fact that they were actually going to get to "grade" their teacher.

The report card was simple and to the point. It had no space for the student's name, as the best way to get honest feedback from students is to allow them to express themselves anonymously. Questions and prompts included:

- ♦ Does my teacher make class interesting? If not, what could she do to make the class more interesting?
- ♦ Does my teacher care about me as a person?
- ♦ Does my teacher hold me accountable for my actions?
- ♦ Am I allowed to contribute my opinions in this class?
- ♦ Does my teacher allow me to actively participate in each lesson?
- ♦ Does my teacher treat all students fairly and with dignity and respect?
- ♦ Am I successful in this class? If not, what could my teacher do to help me to become more successful?
- ♦ Does my teacher enjoy teaching?
- ♦ Do I feel that my teacher is the best teacher she can be?
- ♦ What I like about this class is _____.
- ♦ What I do not like about this class is _____.
- ♦ If I could change one thing about this class, it would be _____.

Each time my students received their report cards, I also received mine. And I can tell you that it was the most useful and honest feedback that I ever received about my teaching.

Allowing your students to "grade" your performance accomplishes several things:

- ♦ It holds you, as their teacher, accountable.
- ♦ It gives a message to students that their opinions matter.
- ♦ It shows students that their input is valued.
- ♦ It keeps you on your toes!

Over the years, as I have shared this idea with teachers of all grade levels and content areas, I have continued to notice that good teachers love the idea and can't wait to implement it. Less effective teachers are less than enthusiastic about the idea of having their students grade them.

Be the most effective teacher you can be, and allow your students to help you become just that. Devise your own teacher report card, and allow your students to provide you with valuable feedback. They will!

Students are looking at all that you do.
They watch, and then they imitate you!

Be a Role Model for Your Students

When we sign a contract and call ourselves "teacher," we have accepted the profound responsibility of being a role model to every one of our students. Students need role models, and they seek them out in their lives. **Think back to your own role models. We all had them. They were the people who cared about you, who encouraged your success, who inspired you to accomplish – people who possessed qualities that you wanted to emulate.** I often tell teachers that their students watch them very closely, and that their actions, of course, speak much louder than their words. As teachers, we often forget just how loudly our actions speak, and we end up modeling the exact opposites of the lessons we're trying to teach our students. It looks something like this:

Teacher yells at a student: "Don't you yell at me, young lady!"

Teacher, with a very unpleasant look, says to a belligerent student: "Take that look off of your face!"

These are actual scenarios of teachers modeling the exact behaviors they were trying to prevent in students! You see, students notice everything. Isn't it true that they notice when you wear a new outfit, when you get a haircut, when you NEED a haircut, when you are not feeling well? And isn't it true that they notice if you treat one student in a more favorable way than other students???

Just in case you are not convinced of how closely your students watch your actions, here is a challenge for you. Walk into your classroom tomorrow and ask, "Would any of you like to imitate me?" They'll imitate you, and they'll do it well! Remember that students may not always do what you say, but they are sure to imitate what you do!

In any classroom, the chances are ample to study the teacher and learn by example!

If the students know they get to you, they're going to keep on trying.
You're selling your reactions, and every student is buying!

Maintain Your Composure

I believe that the BIGGEST mistake any teacher will ever make is one that most teachers make on a daily basis. Here it is: We let students know when they *get to us*. **It's not our feelings that determine who we are to others, but rather our actions.** And one of the most difficult tasks to accomplish as a teacher is the ability to control your actions and maintain your composure at all costs. Yes, students will *try* you. They will *work on your nerves*. They will go *for your jugular*—not because they're bad, but because they're children. And to be able to control an adult's emotions is a very powerful feeling for a child. An important word of advice: Don't play the game. You will feel frustrated at times. That's normal. But to roll your eyes, clench your teeth when you speak, fold your arms and tap your foot as you stare at the ceiling, sigh, raise your voice, or exhibit any of the many signs of a loss of composure will only serve to let students know that you <u>did</u> play, you <u>did</u> lose, and you gave your control over to them. You can be serious without looking angry. You can discipline a child in a thoughtful, professional manner. You see, there is never an appropriate time to *lose your cool*. You are a professional, and you must act as a professional at all times. Therefore, you must never let them see you sweat. When students realize that you will not play the game and that you are truly a professional, they will stop trying to see how red they can make your face get, how far that vein in your neck will stick out… You will, in turn, earn their respect, but most importantly, you will serve as the role model that so many of them so desperately need.

Never dig yourself a hole by losing hold of self-control!

*Even if you sometimes view your
administrator as a dictator,
The time you spend complaining
about your administrator should
not be greater
Than the actual time you spend in
the presence of said administrator.
Try to be a cooperator as opposed
to another problem creator.*

Cooperate with Administration

I often hear teachers complaining about their administrators. I typically listen for a while and then ask, "What percentage of the school day do you typically spend in your classroom with your students?" The answer is usually about 90%. Then I ask, "What percentage of the day do you spend in the presence of your administrator?" The answer is usually 1% or less, unless, of course, the teacher is married to his or her administrator, and since I'm not a marriage counselor, I leave immediately! The fact remains that some teachers spend a good percentage of their time complaining about someone they hardly see. Wouldn't it make more sense to put 100% of your efforts into the people with whom you spend more than 90% of your school day?

It will never happen that all of the teachers agree with administrative decisions all of the time. If you feel strongly about a particular issue, then you should discuss it privately and professionally with your administrator. But if the issue is one over which you have no control, let it go. I once knew a teacher who spent a considerable amount of her time griping about the dress code policy. She wanted to wear blue jeans, and the policy forbade it. She allowed that one issue to consume her. In anger, she turned against the administrator and refused to support any of his decisions. This, of course, was unprofessional. It affected her entire personality, so the students suffered also.

In a truly effective school, teachers work together in cooperation with administration. They don't always agree with administration, yet they support administrative decisions, as much as possible, for the betterment of the school and ultimately the students. Don't get caught up in petty issues that lead to breakdowns in communication and cooperation. Remember, as discussed in Tip 69, to focus on what you CAN change—not on what you CAN'T. When we focus our efforts on working cooperatively toward a common goal—helping children—we may not always agree, but our students will always benefit.

No one should find it curious that if you act when you are furious, Anger is what you'll send out and anger is what you'll get. What you do out of anger is exactly what you will eventually regret!

Avoid "Acting When Angry"

We've all been there. We can remember the feeling of boiling blood pulsing through our veins, building, racing through our bodies, and then—BANG—an explosion! We got angry, and we lost control. We said things that, to this day, we still regret. How we wish we could take it all back. Well, we can't. And the bad news is that we've probably all been guilty of not learning a lesson from it. We get angry again, and we act or speak without thinking. Once again, we lament the fact that we allowed ourselves to give in to the anger. We are all human; we all have emotions; we all experience anger. But not everyone expresses anger in the same way. As stated in Tip 65, **our feelings don't determine how others perceive us, but our actions surely do.**

A teacher stood in front of her classroom and "warned" her students several times to stop talking. They would stop for a few minutes, and then the talking would resume. Since I was seated in the back of the room, I watched her getting angrier with each warning. Her face became redder, her breathing became labored, her body became tense, and finally, she exploded. She threw her book down and began scream- ing. She then went into a tirade that she later regretted. But she couldn't take it back.

We often hear it suggested that when angry, we should *count to 10* or do some- thing to calm ourselves in order to avoid saying or doing something we'll later regret. Anger is a very powerful emotion. And in the classroom, it can be a very dangerous emotion if we do not control it. Just as we try to teach students to recognize their anger for what it is and to avoid losing control, so must we, as their teachers and role models, model appropriate ways of dealing with difficult situations. It is never appropriate to lose control of your emotions in the classroom. **When you're so angry that you can't think straight, you're right—you can't think straight.** Wait until you can, and think about how you will handle the situation from a logical perspective.

Take a deep breath, think things through, and never allow anger to be in control of you!

FACT: If you do not have personal problems, then you are not a person. However, if you allow your personal problems to spill over into your classroom, then you are not a professional!

Do Not Allow Your Personal Problems to Spill Over into the Classroom

I once heard a teacher announce to her class, "Look, I'm having a bad day. I've been up all night with a sick child, so I'm not in a good mood. I'm going to try to concentrate on my teaching, but I'm tired. Also, we've fallen way behind in the textbook, so we're going to have to move fast today. Stay in your seats, and don't mess with me!"

Now imagine an airline pilot in a similar situation. "This is your pilot speaking, and boy, am I having a bad day! I've been up all night with a sick child, so I'm not in a good mood. I'm going to try to get you to New York, but I'm tired, so I'm not promising you anything. Also, we've fallen way behind on our schedule, so we're going to have to fly extra fast! So sit in your seats, and don't mess with me!"

What would you do as a passenger on this plane? You'd deplane, immediately, even in mid flight! The fact is that students don't have the luxury of getting out of your classroom. However, they would feel the same way, in your classroom, that you would feel on that flight. Teachers are human, and so it is normal for them to experience human trials and tribulations. What is not normal is to allow those struggles to affect their students.

I'm sure that somewhere out there, there are pilots who are not having the best of days. The trick is never to allow their bad days to affect their passengers. And so it should be in the classroom. **Students are not vents for our frustrations.** If you're having a day that is so bad that you feel you cannot teach, then stay home. If you choose to come to school, however, be a professional! All "passengers" in your classroom should enjoy a safe flight and an on-time arrival.

Try to control what's uncontrollable and soon you will be inconsolable!

Focus on What You CAN Change

Okay, so your administrator does not always see things the way you see them. Maybe the school's cafeteria food will never be classified as gourmet, the school custodian may miss a spot or two on occasion, and parents may not rear their children in ways that meet with your standards. But what does that have to do with what goes on within the four walls of your classroom? Very little, if anything. The fact is that **many people spend most of their time focusing on things they simply cannot change.** As teachers, we must learn to place 100% of our energies on things we can do something about. And we can absolutely do something about the teaching and learning that takes place in our classrooms every day. The following are examples of teachers focusing needless energy on things they can do very little about:

♦ "I met Brandon's parents yesterday, and now I understand why he's like he is. He doesn't stand a chance."

♦ "Why is it that our principal won't allow us to wear jeans?"

♦ "Did you hear what Mrs. _____ told her students today?"

♦ "How can they expect us to teach from this textbook?"

♦ "Have you noticed the way that Mr. _____ looks at Ms. _____? I think there's something going on."

♦ "Kids today are just not what they used to be."

♦ "How I wish I had my time in. I'd retire today."

All right, I think you get the point. A good rule is this: When faced with a problem at school, ask yourself, "Is there anything I can do to remedy this situation? If so, what's my plan of action?" If your answer is no, then let it go. If your answer is yes, then DO something!

Focus on things that you can change and never on those you cannot.
And help your students to learn and to grow. They need you.
They need you a lot!

*The day you finish learning to teach is the
day you should retire,
For in the classroom of a stagnant teacher,
the situation is dire.
The fact remains that no one has ever
learned all there is to know,
So seize every available opportunity to
continue to learn and grow!*

Grow as a Professional

I've often heard it said that some teachers teach 30 years, and others teach one year 30 times! Education is like the field of medicine. We are constantly discovering new and better ways of doing things. Therefore, we must continue to learn and search and question.

*A superintendent told me that he requires ALL of his 2000 teachers to write professional growth plans, every year. These plans include the teachers' yearly goals for improvement. The plans are monitored and are then evaluated at the end of the year. "This ensures that ALL of my teachers are constantly getting better," he said, "We don't expect perfection, but we insist on improvement." When asked about why the goals were written and evaluated, he said, "**It's a fact that people who have specific written goals are far more successful than those who have vague mental goals.** That's why we also have district-wide goals, and they're posted in every classroom. We have a definite direction, and everyone is headed that way." When I asked a teacher in this district about her professional growth plan, she responded, "I wasn't crazy about the idea at first. It seemed like just one more thing we had to do, and I already had plenty enough to do. But having these goals keeps me sharp. I set them, and then I move toward them. And I always arrive at my destination a much more competent teacher."*

For more on goal setting, see Tip 58.

***If, through teaching, a living you are earning
Then stoke the fire of learning in yourself and keep it burning!***

Motivation and Rapport

Teacher, When You Lit a Spark in Me...

Teacher, when you lit a spark in me, my very best you soon did see
And once I was convinced that you cared, I worked much harder
*   and I even dared*
To chance the obstacles I used to avoid
For fear that my pride would be destroyed
I learned, from you, that I could do it
You challenged me and saw me through it
And when I fell, you lifted me
With your clever ways, you gifted me
With the knowledge that falling was a step to success
And at times, I doubted you, I must confess
But retrospect provides clear sight
And I write this poem now in hopes that you might
Understand the tremendous influence you had
On a little boy once construed as bad
He's all grown now and successful too
And he owes so much of that to you!

A.L.B.

I'm Not My Older Brother

I'm not my older brother, so please do not compare
To treat me as another would surely be unfair
He has ways of doing things—ways that are his own
He's okay, but there's no way that I'll become his clone
I'm not my older brother, and I do not wish to be
I'm happy to be who I am, and that is simply me.

A.L.B., *101 Poems for Teachers*

Celebrate the Uniqueness of Your Students

Said a mother of her identical twins, "They grew up at the same time in the same home with the same parents, yet they are polar opposites! Go figure." Every child is his own person with unique talents, skills, strengths, and dreams. Remember this in the classroom! **Don't ever compare students to their siblings or to other students. Rather, find the unique aspects of each student and celebrate those qualities.** I am not, of course, referring to a student's unique quality of being the most disruptive person in the classroom. Not exactly a cause for celebration... Find the strengths and talents in each student, and nurture those.

A high school student once told me, "The thing I like best about Mr. C is that he doesn't compare me to my brothers. I'm the youngest of six boys, and they've all gone to this same school. So every year, I'm known by most of my teachers as the last of the Patterson boys. We all look alike, so they expect that we all ARE alike, and we're not. I like my brothers, all right, but I don't want to walk in their footsteps. I've got my own path mapped out. Anyway, Mr. C never even mentions my brothers, and he's taught them all. He just acts as if I'm a regular guy, my own person."

Remember that each student is a unique individual, his own person. Treat him that way. Celebrate who he is rather than pushing him to be someone he's not.

To put it in its simplest terms: *I am me. I am not you. If you should think that I am you, please see me.*

The teacher who is attempting to teach without inspiring the pupil with a desire to learn is hammering on cold iron.

Horace Mann

Light a Spark in Your Students

I cannot think of a more simplified way to stress the importance of lighting a spark in your students than by saying the following: **What really matters is not so much what students walk away with in their *hands*, but rather how many sparks were ignited in their *hearts*.** Students don't want more *stuff*. They want *inspiration*. And it takes talent to inspire. That's why it is the TEACHER who is the key to the success of the students in the classroom. The TEACHER, not the CONTENT, determines whether students walk away *ignited* or *extinguished*.

I recently spoke with a seventh-grade student who had been retained three times. The student readily told me that he had never liked school because he just wasn't any good at it—that was, he said, until he encountered Mrs. Thomas, his seventh-grade teacher. From the beginning of the school year, he felt inspired. He felt successful. He could hardly believe the feeling, as it was one he had never experienced in school. His grades soared, and he soon caught up with his classmates—so much so that the school decided to move him on to the ninth grade. The following is a quote from this student: "Being in Mrs. Thomas' class was like a dream come true. She made learning fun, and she found some talents in me that no one else had ever noticed. Had I had Mrs. Thomas years ago, I would probably be in the right grade today. I'm not a failure. I guess I just needed to be inspired."

Would that we could all be Mrs. Thomases. And we can. Light a spark in all of your students. Set them aglow with a desire to work harder, to search for answers, to acquire deeper understandings, to love learning, and to be better people. If you can do that, then you have done your job well.

The best teachers inspire and set their students' minds afire!

Surely the world would change, I think,
with a smile on everyone's face
To think that simply a smile or a wink could
make this a happier place.

Smile

"Don't smile until Christmas!" Have you heard it? How about this one: "Be mean until Halloween!" Sadly, there are veteran teachers who can't wait to share this *wisdom* with new teachers. This is anything but wisdom, and it is BAD advice. FACT: **Children need *happy* adults in their lives.** FACT: **A smile is the fastest way to get to a student's heart.**

Imagine sitting in a classroom all day where the teacher never smiles. As a teacher, imagine refraining from smiling for even a day, much less until Christmas! Students need to see their teachers smiling—often! The very best teachers smile most of the time, and sometimes it's fake! They do not, of course, smile at a student who is misbehaving. But the fact that they smile most of the time markedly decreases the times that students are misbehaving.

> *I tried an experiment with a new teacher. She was experiencing difficulties with student behavior. Upon observing her, I noticed that she never smiled one time throughout the lesson. She actually appeared angry. So we agreed that for one day, she would teach with a pleasant demeanor and smile as often as possible. I gave her my phone number and asked her to call me the following night to let me know of the results. The phone rang, and since smiles can literally be heard over the phone, I knew the experiment had worked. "They were so much better behaved today," she said. "And they even asked me what I was so happy about, which told me that I really needed to smile more."*

Will smiling solve ALL behavior problems? No. Will it help to dramatically improve behavior in your classroom? Absolutely. And the best part is that it's free and takes no extra planning! Is your smiling face the first thing students see when they enter your classroom? Is it the last thing they see when they leave?

Smile away and successful you'll be. A happy teacher your students should see. For happy students behave, I'm told. And miserable teachers grow miserably old!

Aerodynamically, the bumblebee shouldn't be able to fly, but the bumblebee doesn't know it, so it goes on flying anyway.

Mary Kay Ash

Give Your Students More Credit than They Deserve

I sat at a teacher's desk one day during an observation. There, written on a note taped to her desk was the following: "My students might not be as good as I lead them to believe they are, but they'll try harder because of it." I couldn't wait to talk to her about this. When I asked her about it, she smiled and said, "That's my philosophy. I believe in giving my students just a little more credit than they deserve, and they always rise to the occasion. If they don't know they can't do something, then their chances of doing it are increased. I believe in helping students to believe in themselves, because once they believe in themselves, they're unstoppable!"

This teacher hit the nail on the head! Tell your students that they're a little better than they are, and they'll become a little better than they are. The key here is "a little." You do not want to tell a student who struggles to write a complete sentence that he is a brilliant writer. Use discretion and a little common sense. There are lots of young bumblebees learning to fly in your classroom. Don't tell them they can't. Let them fly!

I didn't know I couldn't, so I tried and I did
Cleverly, your lack of faith in me you somehow hid
Or maybe it was faith in me that somehow you possessed
That led you not to let me know—and helped me be my best!

Who's My Teacher's Favorite?

Who's my teacher's favorite? I'm
fairly sure it's me.
What? You think it's you instead?
That simply cannot be.
Of course, now that you mention it,
she treats us both the same.
She smiles at me, she smiles at you;
she calls us both by name;
She helps me when I'm struggling;
she does the same with you;
She helps us to be better at whatever
we're trying to do;
With any classroom rules she has,
she makes us both comply;
And when we feel like giving up, she encourages us to try.
So who's her favorite student, then? Neither of us can deny
That unmistakably, unequivocally, it seems to be a tie!

A.L.B., *101 Poems for Teachers*

Make Every Student Your "Favorite"

I often tell teachers that if I should walk into their classrooms and ask the students who their teacher's favorite student is, all hands should go up. If a few hands remain down, I can practically guarantee that those are the students causing problems. **Students who do not feel that you care are the ones most likely to seek your attention in inappropriate ways.** The good news is that the opposite is also true. Once a student of any age level is convinced that you care about him, he will do almost anything to please you. He will act politely, do his work, behave appropriately, and even turn in homework! It's quite simple: Students want to feel successful, appreciated, and respected. And though the task is no small one, you should make it a priority to make each student feel that he is your "secret favorite." You can accomplish this by taking a personal interest in every student, making sure that each is experiencing success, and doing all the little things that tell them you care. Show me a teacher who treats all students as "favorites" and I'll show you a classroom with few behavior problems and high levels of student achievement!

> *If you would win a man to your cause, first*
> *convince him that you are his sincere friend.*
> Abraham Lincoln

When you tell a student he can do it,
and you show him how and see him
through it,
Usually he'll do it and he'll succeed.
Success—it breeds success indeed!

Set the Stage for Success

Nathan was fifteen years old and in the seventh grade. On the day he arrived, he announced to me that he was there only because he had been expelled from his previous school and that he had no intentions of learning anything. He was simply biding his time until he could quit school. I knew I had to do something to make him successful, and the sooner the better! "By the way," he added, "you have a nice car." Bingo! He liked cars. He already knew which teacher drove what car. I began to allow him to teach me everything he knew about cars. In class, I used every opportunity to relate what I taught him to cars and engines. We started at his level, which was quite low, and he steadily improved. (See Tip 30 for more on teaching students at their level.) As often as possible, we read and wrote about cars. Soon he was telling ME how a particular skill reminded him of something to do with cars, engines, motorcycles, etc. He was experiencing success in school, possibly for the first time in his life. The rest of the story is that not only did he remain in school, but he went on to receive a high school diploma. No small feat for Nathan! Then, some years later, I was filling my gas tank at a local convenience store when I heard a deep voice say, "How about a hug?" It was Nathan! He was now a successful auto mechanic earning a salary higher than mine!

It is true that nothing breeds success like success. However, many students do not experience much success in school. This does not have to be the case. One of our main jobs, as teachers, is to help all students experience success so as to spur them onward toward more success. Nathan was a perfect example. He simply needed to experience success. In some way, every student is Nathan. And every time he experiences the tiniest taste of success, he'll be hungry for more.

If success breeds success, then help me succeed
And from that success, more success will breed
And I'll become successful, which is what I need
So do what it takes, please, to help me succeed!

Tip 76

I can live for two months on a good compliment.

Mark Twain

Provide Positive Feedback

Research has concluded, time and again, that **it takes several positive comments to neutralize one negative comment in the eyes of a student.** However, in the typical school, negative comments far outweigh positive ones. We are all aware of the fact that positive environments are far more conducive to student cooperation and achievement than are negative environments. Yet many classrooms often resonate with the sounds of "Don't do that," "Stop it," "Be quiet," "Pay attention," "Sit up straight," "Go to the office," etc.

In an attempt to see if it was possible to turn this situation around, I, along with one of my coworkers, conducted an experiment. The experiment I'm about to share with you has produced amazingly positive results in every one of the 20 plus schools in which we've attempted it thus far. Here's how it works. I conduct a brief faculty in-service, sharing the information I have just shared with you regarding the typical ratio of *positive* to *negative* comments in classrooms. Then I ask the faculty for permission to conduct an experiment with them, expressing my expectations that they will defy the research. They always agree to the experiment. I tell them that my coworker and I will visit their classrooms, and that we will simply be keeping a tally of positives and negatives. We will give credit for smiles, praise, constructive feedback to students, positive sayings on the walls, any type of positive comment made to students, etc. One stipulation is that students will not be made aware of what is going on. I also tell them the date that we will be conducting the experiment, and it never fails—one or two teachers approach me afterward and say, "You shouldn't have told everyone which day you were coming. Some of them are very negative, and they'll just fake being positive on the day that you're here." I always thank them for their concern and assure them that all will be fine. You see, I am intentionally setting them up for success, but they don't yet realize that. (See Tip 76.)

On the day of the experiment, it is typical to identify a ratio of anywhere from 25-50 positive comments to every one negative. It is also very typical that on that day, student office referrals drop drastically. It's amazing! Teachers are smiling, students are smiling, and learning is evident. I then compile the results and return to speak to the faculty. I begin by congratulating them on their positive school environment. I provide nothing but positive feedback, and they all beam with pride. They are always amazed at how well behaved the students were, especially since the students were not even aware of the experiment. And then the real lesson: I share with them the fact that several of them seemed concerned that my announcing the date of the experiment would sway the results of the experiment. Then I say, "I have just taught you a very powerful lesson about teaching. I set you up for success. I told you the date of the experiment, knowing that you would make a special effort to be positive. You see, I didn't want to *catch* you doing something negative. Had I done that with a *surprise attack* experiment, the results may not have been quite as positive. Then, had I provided negative feedback, insisting that you change your attitudes, you would have become defensive and resentful. Instead, I set you up for success so that I could provide you with some useful, positive feedback. I simply wanted to prove to you that being positive makes a BIG difference. And remember, the only thing that was different was YOUR attitude, YOUR approach. The students had no idea what was going on, but they responded favorably to the positive environments in your classrooms."

"This," I tell them, "is how you want to approach your teaching. Set your students up for success by maintaining a positive attitude, providing positive feedback, and expressing your belief in each student's abilities."

Oh, and something else that never fails: The assistant principals (who usually handle the discipline referrals) always ask me to come back the next day, and the next day, and the next!

Express belief and you'll eventually SEE it.
Tell me I AM and then watch me BE it!

A Very Clever Teacher

We had to draw a picture one day, but I
*   couldn't decide what to draw,*
So I decided to leave my paper blank, and
*   my teacher looked at it in awe.*
"What a beautiful fluffy white cloud!" she
*   said, "May I hang it on the wall?"*
And I realized that she did not notice that I
*   had drawn nothing at all.*
Then she proudly hung for all to see the
*   work I had not done,*
But with her permission I took it home and
*   I added the sky and the sun.*
And now that I think about it, I wonder if
*   she really knew*
That my drawing was not of a cloud at all;
*   it was work that I did not do.*
I thought that I had tricked her, but maybe
*   it was she*
Who used a clever way to get me to draw a
*   picture for all to see.*

                                    A.L.B.

Use Clever Psychology

Tip 78

How many teachers truly utilize the kind of psychology that the teacher in the above poem uses? Many do, but many others do not. The general rule is: The teacher gives an assignment, the child turns in a blank paper, and the child gets an F. Not very conducive to improving student achievement! The fact is that **with the right psychology, you can get a child to do just about anything.**

Liz Yates, one of the most positive teachers I have ever had the privilege of knowing, went into a classroom to observe a new teacher. The teacher was having problems with a particular student and was willing to try anything. Liz spotted the student immediately. She was a tall, over-aged student, and she had a way of making her presence known, to put it mildly. She was out of her seat, walking around, blurting out answers, picking on other students, etc. Following the observation, Liz asked the teacher for permission to speak to this student. Liz called the student out of the room, and the student followed, surmising that she was in trouble. Liz introduced herself and said to the student, "I'm Mrs. Yates, and I work for the school board. I couldn't help noticing some things about your behavior." Now the student really assumed that she was in trouble! Liz went on to say, "I noticed that you have a way of standing out in a crowd. You've got some real leadership potential!" The student, dumbfounded, listened attentively. "I also noticed," said Liz, "that you're very knowledgeable." (You see, she had noted that even though the student was blurting out answers, the answers were correct!) "Have you ever thought about being a teacher when you grow up?" asked Liz. "You know, if you could learn to temper your behavior a little, I think that both you and others would really benefit from your skills and abilities. You've got some real possibilities." The student thanked Liz profusely and went back into the classroom. Liz told the teacher about how she had handled the situation, and the teacher decided to give that same psychology a try. Months later, Liz went back into that classroom. The student ran up to Liz, called her by name, hugged her, and said, "I've decided to be a teacher, and I've really been practicing hard!" The teacher told Liz that the child had become a model student. "She participates in class, she behaves very well, she's working on managing her tendency to express her opinions inappropriately, and she now stays in at recess to tutor the same students she used to tease. I can't believe the difference, and I'm amazed at what a little psychology can accomplish!" said the teacher.

Using clever psychology can be both fascinating and fun! Of course, **the right psychology requires the right attitude.** Any effective teacher will tell you that *attitude* will make or break you in the classroom. So adopt the attitude of helping students to help themselves. Be resolved to turn potentially negative situations into positive ones. Model an attitude of optimism. Convince students that you believe in them—especially when they are having trouble believing in themselves. You have nothing to lose, and your students have everything to gain. Be careful of the attitude you choose, and save your students pain and brain drain.

Enthusiasm Is Contagious

Be careful about your enthusiasm; it
spreads like chicken pox
It may cause your students to answer the
door when opportunity knocks
Your enthusiasm spills onto them and they
become infected
And to date no one has found an antidote to
be injected
To remove this love of learning once it
enters a student's brain
Is like trying to stop the rainbow from
appearing after rain
So be careful about how happy and how
excited you are about teaching
For soon your love of learning will become
much too far-reaching
For you to ever contain the influence you
have upon this Earth
So consider yourself forewarned about
displaying too much mirth!

A.L.B., *101 Poems for Teachers*

Act as though Every Subject You Teach Is Your "Favorite"

How often have we heard a teacher say to students, "Well, word problems were never my favorite either, but we have to do them, so let's grin and bear it." Once I heard a teacher say to her class, "Look, I'm not very good at writing essays either, so we'll be learning together." Imagine a doctor saying to you, the patient, "Look, your particular illness is my least favorite to treat, but you're sick, so let's see what we can do . . ." or better yet, "I'm not a very good surgeon so we'll be learning together!" Now please do not misunderstand. I am in no way suggesting that *acting* enthusiastic is enough. No *enthusiastic* surgeon will operate on me unless he is qualified! However, I do want to feel that my qualified surgeon enjoys what he does and thereby continues to improve his skills. By the same token, acting enthusiastic in the classroom is not enough. You must be, of course, qualified to teach the subject matter. However, being qualified without being enthusiastic will not make for successful teaching. It is true that every subject we teach may not be our favorite. The trick is not to announce that to your students. You see, student enthusiasm tends to mirror teacher enthusiasm. If you should ever doubt this, follow a group of students from an enthusiastic teacher's classroom to a non-enthusiastic teacher's classroom. You'll witness an entirely different group of students, or so it will seem. So be the most enthusiastic person you know with whatever you teach.

Aside from being scholastic, if you want to be fantastic, you've got to be enthusiastic!

Keep your face to the sunshine and you cannot see the shadows.
Helen Keller

Focus on the "Positives" in Your Classroom

I once watched a speaker make a profound statement to his audience with the use of an activity. He had the audience look around the room. They had thirty seconds to locate and memorize everything they saw that was yellow. The activity began, and everyone scanned the room for yellow objects. After thirty seconds, he had them close their eyes. He then said, "Now make a mental list of everything in this room that is black." The participants, stunned, could not remember one thing that was black. (Their eyes were still closed.) He then had them open their eyes and look around. They were amazed that there were many more black objects than yellow. However, since they had focused on yellow, that's all they had seen. Point? "Keep your face to the sunshine (yellow) and you cannot see the shadows (black)." The speaker made the profound point that life is what we focus on. I will relate that same principle to the classroom. In our classrooms, at any given time, there are negatives (black) and there are positives (yellow). If we look hard enough, we will find something negative, if that's where we place our focus. The good news is that the same holds true for the positives in our classrooms. It can be easy, at times, to get frustrated and begin focusing on all that's wrong. These are phrases you will hear in the classroom of someone focusing on negatives: "Don't do that." "Sit down." "Sit up straight." "Stop it." "Pay attention!" "Get quiet." "Don't make me send you to the principal." Interestingly, students do tend to live up to the expectations of their teachers, so inappropriate behaviors are actually being encouraged in this type of classroom. Conversely, these are phrases you will hear often in the classroom of someone focusing on positives: "Thank you for raising your hand." "Great job!" "I appreciate your attentiveness to this important task." "I'm so proud of you." Once again, students tend to meet our expectations, so in this case, positive behaviors are being encouraged. This is not to suggest that nothing negative ever happens in the classroom of a positive teacher. However, these incidences are rare and are dealt with in a respectful manner. Once again, this encourages positive behaviors.

Effective teachers know that focusing on positive behaviors will foster positive behaviors. So focus on the yellow and obliterate the black!

Around the room, my teacher displayed the projects that we all had made
And pictures of us adorned the wall, and some of our work samples hung in the hall
And happy we were and harder we tried—for we were the source of our teacher's pride!

Display Student Work

During a visit to a ninth-grade science class, I immediately noticed that the classroom walls consisted of lots of student work and pictures of students working. The teacher said to the students, "Tell Ms. Breaux about what we've been learning." They began pointing to their projects around the room and their work samples on the walls. After I remarked about one particular project, a student quickly led me to the pictures taken while the students were completing the project—a photographic display of every step of the process. The students wanted to show me everything and tell me about all they had been doing. One of the students even suggested getting a photograph of them explaining their work to me. The teacher readily picked up his camera and snapped a few shots while the students continued to speak of their accomplishments. Then one student said, "Oh, let me show a picture of the experiment that didn't work." He quickly led me to a photograph, and beneath it was a poster titled, "What We Learned from This Mistake."

When I was speaking with the teacher afterward, he told me that the classroom belonged to everyone, so he believed in giving everyone equal ownership. "Notice," he said, "that everyone has work displayed. That's because every student experiences success in my class. But also notice that there are no graded assignments on the walls. If I did that, only the brightest students would have their work displayed. I want everyone's work up there, and they all want their work up there, too. For some, it's the first time they've ever had any of their work showcased. I've also noticed that the more pictures I take, the harder they work. They love to see pictures of themselves working."

When asked what advice he would give to other teachers about displaying student work, he smiled and said, "Display lots of student work in the classroom, and turn every learning opportunity into a 'Kodak' moment."

Treat people as if they were what they ought to be, and you'll help them to become what they are capable of becoming.

Johann Wolfgang von Goethe

Have Positive Expectations for ALL Students

Years back, I had an experience I will never forget. It was the week before school began, and I attended a meeting for parents and teachers. The parents of Raneesha said to me, "We're apologizing in advance for Raneesha's attitude." "What do you mean?" I asked. I had not even met Raneesha yet. "Well, she's got a real attitude problem. Any teacher who's ever taught her can tell you that, and we see it at home every day. We tell her that her attitude is bad, but that doesn't change her. Just let us know when she gets out of line, and we'll deal with her." Knowing that I needed to address that situation from day one, I decided that I would find any opportunity to capitalize on any hint of a positive attitude I could manage to find in Raneesha. I was a little apprehensive about meeting her, yet I was determined to have high expectations. On the first day of school, Raneesha walked into my class. I introduced myself, and she reluctantly shook my hand. I then said, "You look like someone I can trust. Would you please bring this very important envelope to the secretary for me?" (The envelope was empty, and the secretary already knew to expect it.) "Yes," answered Raneesha, with a hint of a smile on her face. "Thank you so much," I responded. "I love your attitude!" I said. From that moment on, Raneesha displayed a model attitude in my class. But I never let up on mentioning her positive attitude to her as often as possible. About six weeks later, Raneesha stayed after class one day to hand me a letter from her parents. "What's this?" I asked. "It's a letter from my parents. They wanted to tell you that my attitude has improved a lot at home, and they want to thank you for helping me with that." Acting totally oblivious to her past history, I said, "What do you mean by improved? How could your attitude possibly improve? You've got one of the best attitudes I've ever seen in a seventh grader." Raneesha went on to explain to me what I already knew—the fact that her attitude had previously left a lot to be desired, both at home and at school. "So why the sudden change?" I asked. "Well, I thought about that a lot," said Raneesha. "Remember on the first day of school when you told me I had a good attitude?

I guess I figured you didn't know any better and that maybe I did have a good attitude hidden inside of me somewhere. You were the first person that ever told me anything positive about my attitude. It was like you just expected me to have a good attitude, so I did."

This is just one small, yet profound, example of how students will live up to your expectations. If you treat students as if you expect them to be successful, whether it is in their studies or in their dealings with others, and if you start with very small successes and capitalize on those as opposed to reinforcing negative expectations, then they will become what they are capable of becoming! **Just as we tend to get out of life what we expect out of life, we tend to get out of our students what we expect out of our students.**

I Wish My Teacher Knew Me

*I wish my teacher knew me. Instead, she
   looks right through me.*
*But if she stopped and looked inside, she'd
   see the good I try to hide.*
*And when she did, she'd be surprised by all
   she never realized*
*And she wouldn't misconstrue me, if only
   my teacher knew me.*

A.L.B.

Get to Know Your Students

Tip 83

A teacher was having problems with a student, and she called for my assistance. She described the problem student—I will call him T.J.—as lazy, tuned-out, uncaring, unfeeling, and disrespectful. He rarely did his work in class and he never did homework. In fact, she had been sending him to the principal, to no avail. "What do you know about his home life?" I asked. "I don't have time to delve into these students' home lives," she responded. "I barely have time to get my work done at school. Besides, I've got enough of my own problems at home." As it turned out, T.J.'s parents were suspected drug dealers. T.J. was living in a small apartment with aunts, uncles, cousins, siblings, and questionable others. T.J.'s bed at night consisted of a board placed over the bathtub! And yet here was a teacher sending him to the principal for not turning in homework. When I told the teacher what I had learned about T.J.'s home life, she was shocked. And she realized that maybe it was with good reason that T.J. was not a model student. "Wow," she said, "and I thought I had problems."

You see, every child has a story. Some stories are good ones and some are tragic. Regardless, it is vital that we attempt to get to know something personal (without prying, of course) about each. Soon, they become real people to us, and we realize that all people, big and little ones, have their own struggles. This makes it easier for us to understand them and to help them. And though we cannot change our students' home lives, we can most certainly help them to have positive, successful experiences in school. T.J. deserved to have a teacher who took an interest in him. He deserved to have a teacher who cared about him as a person. So do all of the other students. No, you cannot know everything there is to know about every student, but knowing *something* about each of them is both easily attainable and highly beneficial.

Effective teachers look inside for the good things students sometimes hide.

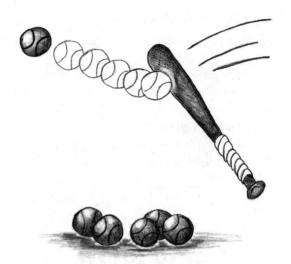

During his career, Babe Ruth hit 714 homeruns. He also struck out 1330 times!

Encourage Improvement, Not Perfection

In the sport of baseball, many, many of the "greats" have made it into the Hall of Fame with a .300 lifetime batting average or less. That means that they *failed* 70% of the time! Yet they are considered extremely successful—the best of the best. In school, however, you have to succeed at least 70% of the time in order to barely get by with a passing grade. Try to imagine ANY area of your life where you are successful more than 70% of the time. I'll bet you'll have a difficult time doing that. In football, every single play is technically designed to score points. However, almost every play does NOT score points. That doesn't stop the coach from attempting to have his team score points on the next play, however. Find a parent who succeeds 70% of the time with everything he tries to teach his child. That parent does not exist. Better yet, find a stockbroker who succeeds with 70% of all of his stock trades! If you do, call me. I'll invest!

The point is that we often label students as failures because we are making the mistake of encouraging perfection in all of them. This is the way we were *trained* to think in school. Admit it—if you took a test with 100 questions and received a grade of 95%, you would immediately look for the five that you missed as opposed to the 95 that you got right! And many of you would be upset with anything less than 100%. In a conversation with a teacher, I learned that she had many students who were experiencing what she called "no success at all." In looking more closely at the situation, I learned that these students were struggling with content that was way above their levels. Amazingly, they were managing to score 50% or better on her tests. I saw some real potential here, and I shared my observations with this teacher. I said, "I'm going to speak to you in Chinese and I'm going to teach you in Chinese and then I'll test you in Chinese. What do you think you'll score?" "Well, I don't know how to speak Chinese, so I'll score a zero," she said. (I don't speak Chinese either, by the way, but I was just trying to make a point.) "Don't you think you could at least get half of all the answers correct?" I asked. "No way," she said. "Well, what you're trying to teach these particular struggling students is material that's far above their levels of understanding. It's almost as if you were speaking and teaching and testing in a language that is foreign to them. Yet they're getting at least half of it correct. Wow! What potential!" I exclaimed. "I never thought of it that way," said the teacher. "I think I see where you're going with this. I need to speak in 'their' language, at 'their' levels." "Absolutely," I answered. "And then move them forward from there. You'll be amazed at their progress, based on their potential and their obvious tendencies to be overachievers!" I added.

The teacher began, the very next day, to teach these students from their current levels of understanding. Then, she agreed that she would focus only on improvement, not perfection. Within a few weeks, these students had made enormous strides. By the end of the semester, each of them was able to pass the course. No, they did not make straight A's, but they did pass. And they were experiencing success unlike they had ever before experienced.

In the classroom, we should teach students that improvement is what matters. Perfection is not only impossible, but striving for it will give you ulcers and will drive the people around you out of their minds! Success is attainable for anyone, one step at a time. Homeruns are great, but strikeouts are opportunities to improve your skills. An enthusiastic "swing and a miss" has led many people to greatness.

The inner landscape of many children is full of mines ready to explode upon careless contact. Any insulting remark can set off an explosion.

Haim Ginott

Avoid Sarcasm

"*What time is it?*" *asked a student.* "*I'll tell you what time it is. It's time for you to be quiet,*" *answered the teacher, in a less than a pleasant tone. Having been seated in the classroom for the past fifteen or so minutes, I knew that this student had been busily and quietly at work.* "*Why the sarcasm?*" *I wondered. A few minutes later, most of the students had finished their assignments. Naturally, some of them began whispering to one another.* "*Excuse me!*" *barked the teacher,* "*You're supposed to be working, not talking.*" "*We're finished,*" *said some of the students.* "*Well, I had better not find any mistakes on your papers,*" *answered the teacher.* "*I can't figure out problem number 4,*" *said another student.* "*Well, maybe if the rest of your classmates would be engaging their brains instead of their mouths, you might be able to concentrate better,*" *huffed the teacher. By this point, almost everyone was talking. The teacher got angrier and became more sarcastic, which finally led to a hostile confrontation with a student.* "*Open your mouth one more time, and you're going straight to the office,*" *yelled the teacher.* "*I'm not going to the office unless everyone else goes,*" *said the student,* "*because they're all talking, too!*"

This situation, of course, went from bad to worse. And this teacher felt victimized by her students. In actuality, however, her negative tone and sarcastic words were provoking the same behaviors in her students—not to mention the fact that there was too much "down" time where students had nothing to do. Therefore, her lack of management led to talking which made her angry and evoked sarcasm. But regardless of what came first, the fact is that this teacher was using sarcasm, and there is simply no place for sarcasm in the classroom. **Sarcasm accomplishes nothing positive, it's completely unprofessional, and it shows a lack of control on the part of the teacher.** Most students in our classrooms have to deal with enough cynicism already in their lives. We, as teachers, are supposed to lift them, build their self-esteem, encourage their endeavors, and model appropriate behavior. Using sarcasm will help to accomplish none of these things. So when is it appropriate to use sarcasm with a student? Never.

What time is it? It's time for all of us to take a good look at our behaviors with students and refrain from using any kind of comments that may even *hint* of sarcasm.

I Never Thought of Her That Way

I saw my teacher shopping in the
*   grocery store today*
What? She shops for groceries? I never
*   thought of her that way*
And I looked inside her basket—and her
*   food was normal too*
She was pushing her basket and walking
*   around like normal people do*
I thought she lived in the classroom—
*   just stayed there night and day*
But it appears that she may just be
*   normal—I never thought of her that*
*   way!*

                                    A.L.B.

Be "Human" to Your Students

If you have ever encountered one of your students in the grocery store or at a social function, then you know that the above poem is true. It's almost as though you're a celebrity when you're recognized by your students outside of school. "Wow! She actually shops for groceries!" Students don't automatically see you as *human*. They see you as their teacher, period. And though there is a fine line that you do not want to cross, you do want to become as human as possible to your students.

In their book, *The First Days of School*, Harry and Rosemary Wong encourage teachers to create a personality bulletin board. All it requires is making a bulletin board about yourself. Items on the bulletin board may include: your hobbies, your interests, pictures of you when you were in school, your school report cards, your family's pictures, awards you have received, your diplomas, etc. It's such a simple idea, and it truly makes a big difference in becoming *human* to your students. Give it a try. Be human to your students, and they will respect you more. Students need to know that you are a living, breathing individual who possibly made less-than-perfect grades when you were in school, too!

Tip 86

Wong, H. K. & Wong, R. T. (2009). *The First Days of School: How to Be an Effective Teacher*. Mountain View, California: Harry K. Wong Publications.

1st person: person speaking (I, me, my, mine, etc.)

2nd person: *person spoken to (you, your, yours, etc.)*

3rd person: *person spoken of (she, he, it, they, etc.)*

Refer to Yourself in the First Person

To emphasize the point I'm trying to make, I'm going to speak to you in the third person. Now imagine that you are in the room with me, and I begin speaking to you in this way: "Ms. Breaux is very glad that you're reading Ms. Breaux's book. She is hoping that it will benefit you in improving your teaching. She really wants you to pay special attention to what is meant by speaking in the first person."

Wouldn't that seem strange that I'm referring to myself almost as if I'm not there or as if I'm speaking of someone else? What comes naturally is to say, "I'm very glad that you're reading my book. I'm hoping that it will benefit you in improving your teaching. I really want for you to pay special attention to what is meant by speaking in the first person."

So why is it that teachers tend to speak to their students using the third person when speaking of themselves? It sounds like this: "Good morning, students. Ms. Breaux wants for you to take out your language books. Ms. Breaux will be showing you how to…" I know you'll recognize it, because it's definitely a *teacher* thing. I have yet to hear anyone in any other profession refer to themselves in the third person. What teachers don't realize is that it sounds condescending and it creates a "distance" or "barrier" between them and their students when they say to a student, "Ms. Breaux is very proud of you," or, "Ms. Breaux doesn't like the way you're behaving." I have found that many teachers do this without thinking about it and without realizing that they are actually modeling incorrect grammar! It's a learned habit. And though I have witnessed this behavior at all grade levels, I have definitely noticed it most in the elementary grades. Give it some thought, and recognize whether or not you tend to speak this way in your classroom. If you do, you may want to rethink it. Speaking in the first person is modeling *natural* speech, and it also makes your conversations with others more personal.

Ms. Breaux is now finished discussing Ms. Breaux's point here.

You Showed a Little Kindness

You showed a little kindness, but to me, the
  act was huge
For instead of humiliating me as my cheeks
  turned the color of rouge
You saw that I had made a mistake and was
  on the verge of tears
And you quickly covered for me as you
  calmed my worst of fears
You said you admired the guts it took for
  me to take a chance
And instead of wanting to crawl in a hole,
  I almost wanted to dance
And though your simple act of kindness
  happened years ago
The difference it made still touches me, and
  I wanted you to know.

                                    A.L.B.

Remember that Little Things Make a Big Difference

FACT: The little things in life make the biggest difference. A simple pat on the back or a smile might be just what someone needs to brighten his day. In the classroom, little things make a big difference to your students. And, by the way, they cost nothing. Here is a list of a few *little things* that will make a *big difference* to your students:

- ◆ Acknowledge student birthdays.
- ◆ Greet each student with a smile as he/she enters your classroom.
- ◆ Compliment students on jobs well done.
- ◆ Make a positive phone call to a parent regarding something his child has accomplished in class.
- ◆ Write encouraging comments on student work.
- ◆ Visit a sick student in the hospital, or at least make a phone call.
- ◆ Write a thank-you note to a student who has given you a gift.
- ◆ Notice haircuts.
- ◆ Attend school functions to show support.
- ◆ Ask students about their hobbies and interests.
- ◆ Notice and encourage even the smallest of student successes.

Though this list is by no means all-inclusive, it reminds us of the little things that we often tend to overlook. **Remember to do the little things, and you will reap the benefits of making big differences in the lives of your students!**

FACT: If you maintain a child's dignity, you will see lasting results. If you take away a child's dignity, you may face lasting revenge.

Dignify Incorrect Responses

In Tip 18, we discussed the importance of avoiding power struggles with students. It has been my observation that teachers often engage in power struggles with students when students either do not know the answer to a question or, better yet, when they give a *ridiculous* answer intentionally. Here's an actual classroom example:

The class was discussing United States presidents. The teacher asked, "Who was our first president?" One student in the back of the room raised his hand and then gave the name of a famous talk-show host. The students, of course, found this quite amusing. The teacher now had a choice. She could enter into a power struggle and show frustration and aggravation, or she could take all energy away from the student, discreetly discouraging that type of answer, maintaining her composure, and still managing to maintain the student's dignity. Had she chosen to play, she would have probably said the following, in a tone of frustration and aggravation: "Very funny. Are you finished with your comedy routine? Now if you can't give serious answers, don't give any at all." This, of course, would have added more fuel to the fire, increasing the likelihood of the same behavior in the future. However, this teacher amazed me as she looked at the student reassuringly and said, "I know exactly what you're thinking. You're thinking of a male, and both the talk-show host you mentioned and the first president are males, and you're thinking of a famous person, and both of these men are famous. Good thinking. Now can someone tell me the name of the first president?" What happened was that another student answered correctly, and the student with the sarcastic answer was completely defused. He looked a little shocked, thinking that his answer was not so far off after all, as his teacher had just given him some credit. For the remainder of the discussion, he remained actively involved, and on two occasions, he volunteered correct answers.

Following the lesson, I commended the teacher on the way she had handled that situation. She said, "Oh, well he's a new student, and he's just trying to fit in. So I'm going to do my best to see that he does fit it, but in a positive way. Besides that, I never give any energy to those kinds of things. I've got bigger fish to fry!"

On the very same day, I was observing in another classroom where one of the students gave an incorrect answer, but not an intentionally incorrect answer. This teacher responded by saying, "We've been talking about this for a week now. Where have you been?" I was appalled, but more important was the fact that this poor student was embarrassed. What this student did for the rest of the class period was absolutely nothing. She shut down completely and was reprimanded once again by the teacher. This time, it was for being inattentive.

When students shut down, we lose them. And if we are the cause of that *shutting down*, then we are facing inevitable discipline problems atop the inevitable academic problems. Students may give incorrect answers, but at least they're participating! And those incorrect answers assist us in monitoring their understanding or lack of understanding of a concept. The secret is to dignify incorrect responses, whether those answers are intentional or not. **When students feel that they are treated with respect and dignity, teachers see lasting, positive results. When the opposite is the case, teachers are setting themselves up to face lasting revenge.**

You nag nag nag nag
And I gag gag gag gag
What a drag drag drag drag
When you nag nag nag nag.

Avoid Nagging

The best way to describe *nagging* is by defining it in teacher terms. Nagging means taking way too long to make a point that could have been stated in a few words. Here's an example:

> *A student has had difficulty turning in homework assignments. One day, she brings in an assignment on time. A "nagging" teacher says, "Mary, why can't you bring in your assignments on time every day? If you can do it once, you can do it again. Doesn't it feel good to have your assignment turned in on time? If you would only do this every time, I wouldn't have to punish you and constantly be on your back about it. Then we'd both be happier. I'm hoping you've learned a lesson from this. Have you?"*

Do you notice how the teacher goes on and on and on? That's nagging. Now let's look at the same situation from a non-nagging standpoint: *"Great, Mary. Thanks for bringing your assignment in on time. I'm so proud of you."* This scenario is an example of encouraging the student as opposed to nagging the student. Students respond much better to encouragement than they do to nagging. (So do adults!) Now, in order not to sound like I'm nagging you about nagging, I'll end this section since I've made my point!

Laughing

Laughing, laughing, wonderful laughter
You laugh so hard that your stomach hurts after
Now each time you think of it the laughter returns
And while laughing you lose sight of all your concerns
So think of it often and laugh laugh laugh
For laughter cuts life's troubles in half.

A.L.B.

Laugh with Your Students

Many studies have been conducted on laughter and many books have been written on the subject. Basically, they all say the same thing: Laughter is the best medicine! It has been proven that laughing releases endorphins in the brain that boost our immune systems and make us happier. Laughing feels good. Environments where laughter abounds are happy places. I once read a study that showed that on the average, children laugh several hundred times a day as opposed to adults who laugh less than twenty! Maybe that's why children are happier and healthier than adults! Students love teachers who laugh with them. Yes, there are times when laughter is not appropriate. That's common sense. But when the opportunity presents itself—and it will present itself often in the classroom—have a good laugh with your students.

Regrettably, many teachers will readily admit that they don't laugh very often in the classroom. I once asked a teacher why she felt this was so, and she answered, "Because teaching is serious business!" Needless to say, she was struggling desperately with managing student behavior. The students weren't having fun *with* the teacher, so they decided to have fun *without* her! You were supposed to laugh at that. Did you?

Tip 91

Is your glass half empty or half full???

Be an Optimist

Consider the following two poems, and decide whether your glass is half empty or half full...

Oh, Woe is Me

Oh, woe is me, I am a teacher—parent, doctor, therapist, preacher,
Battling daily with the youth, whose attitudes are more than uncouth.
A disciplinarian, no stranger to force; don't talk to me after 3:30—I'm hoarse.
One year of experience 20 times o'er; I teach each year like the year before.
My students are disrespectful and lazy, yet they look at me like I am crazy.
If it weren't for students, my life would be swell, and my job wouldn't seem like a
    living hell.
Speaking of which, I've gotta go. My principal's coming—gotta put on a show!

                      A.L.B.

I Teach

I light a spark in a darkened soul, I warm the heart of one grown cold,
I look beyond and see within—behind the face, beneath the skin,
I quench a thirst, I soothe a pain, I provide the food that will sustain,
I touch, I love, I laugh, I cry. Whatever is needed, I supply.
Yet more than I give, I gain from each. I am most richly blessed—I teach!

                      A.L.B.

The choice is YOURS! Be an OPTIMIST!

*The deepest principle of human nature is
the craving to be appreciated.*
William James

Thank Your Students Often

In Tip 88, we discussed the fact that little things make a big difference to students. Saying "thank you" is one of the little things we can do that will make a big difference. Here are some of the benefits of saying "thank you": it's free, it tells students that you care, it makes students feel appreciated and special, it models appropriate manners, it encourages students to do better and to be better, it sets a tone of encouragement in the classroom, and it promotes a positive learning environment.

I had the privilege of observing a teacher who thanks her students more often than any teacher I've ever observed. Here are some of the statements I heard during this observation:

- *"Thank you for getting to work so quickly."*
- *"Thank you for sharing that with us."*
- *"Thank you for understanding that we cannot chew gum in class." (This was said to a student who WAS chewing gum. The student immediately disposed of the gum.)*
- *"Thank you for not bringing the problems from recess into the classroom. I know it's a really difficult thing to do. If you want to discuss it, we'll do that after class. Thanks for understanding that." (This was said to a student who WAS bringing his problems from recess into the classroom. He immediately got quiet.)*
- *"Thank you for that answer."*
- *"Thank you for making that mistake. We can all learn from it."*
- *"Thank you for remembering to bring in your homework."*
- *"Thanks for your help."*

Not surprisingly, this teacher had almost zero discipline problems. Is it any wonder? And yet, she taught lots of *tough* students every year. In her classroom, however, her students were successful, they were polite, they worked diligently, and they absolutely loved her.

Saying "thank you" doesn't cost a thing, yet priceless are the rewards it will bring!

A Teacher's Influence

My Teacher of Many Years Ago

My teacher of many years ago influences me today
The things that she instilled in me have never gone away
In fact, they are a part of every fiber of my being
The blood that courses through me and the eyes through which I'm seeing
The love that I am giving; the decisions that I'm making
The things that I've accomplished and the ones I'm undertaking
For once someone influences you, they live inside your heart
And so of all I am today, my teacher is a part.

A.L.B., *101 Poems for Teachers*

A teacher affects eternity; he can never tell where his influence stops.

Henry B. Adams

Recognize the Importance of Your Influence

Most teachers choose the teaching profession due to the influence of teachers who inspired them somewhere along the way. And **plentiful are the stories of children's lives being positively impacted and sometimes literally saved because of the influence of a teacher.** I know that I would not have chosen the teaching profession, nor would I be writing this book, were it not for the influence of my fourth-grade teacher, Sr. Naoma Duhe; my fifth-grade teacher, Sr. Martha Richard; and my ninth-grade English teacher, Mrs. Marge Barker. They influenced not only the person I was then, but the person I am now and the person that I will become. You see, whether we deserve it or not, our students think that we *hang the moon*, unless we give them reason to believe otherwise. Please don't give them reason to believe otherwise. If you teach a student one day, you live in that student's heart forever. That's almost scary, isn't it? Recognize that if you impact the life of one student in a positive way, you therefore influence the person that he becomes. That influence will affect the life of every person he ever encounters. You will never fully realize the magnitude of your influence. But know, today and every day, that all of your actions and reactions with your students will determine the type of influence you will have on them—not just for today, but for the rest of their lives. Thus, be very aware of the power of your influence.

You become an important part of every student you teach, and so you never really know how far your influence will reach.

Tip 94

A child's life is like a piece of paper on which every passerby leaves a mark.

Chinese Proverb

Realize that You Will Affect Lives

As teachers—as everyday, normal, run-of-the-mill individuals—we often tend to underestimate the fact that we truly do affect the lives of every student we teach. In Tip 94, we discussed your influence on students' lives. This influence can be very powerful—hopefully in a positive sense—yet it can also be very harmful if we do not treat this *power* with the utmost reverence and respect. You see, it is often easy to say things out of frustration—things that we may think nothing of, but that students will internalize and take to heart.

> *A teacher recently shared an experience with me. She said, "I'm an accomplished musician. I teach at the university level; I perform, and I have been quite successful in my career. Isn't it sad that I cannot even balance a checkbook? And it's all because of my fifth-grade teacher." "What do you mean?" I asked. "Well," she said, "I remember it like it was yesterday. I was standing at the board, struggling to work through a math problem. The teacher was so frustrated with me, and she let the whole class know it. She told me I would never be any good at math. Guess what! I never was. It affected me so intensely that I developed a mental block when it came to math, and I've struggled with it all my life."*

Ironically, she recently received a letter from one of her former music students who said, "How often we underestimate the power of words. I will never forget the five words you spoke to me which have stayed with me all my life. The words were, 'I'm so proud of you.'" So from one individual's story comes a perfect example of both the positive and the negative power of a teacher's influence.

Tip 95

If your students believe that in them you believe, your effect will be positive on their futures and what they achieve!

The mediocre teacher tells. The good teacher explains. The superior teacher demonstrates. The great teacher inspires.

William Arthur Ward

Remember Your "Favorite" Teacher

Call up a mental image of your all-time favorite teacher. We all had one. Got it? You're probably already smiling at this point. Now before you read any further, make a list of several characteristics of that teacher, including what made him/her your favorite. Do not read on until you do this.

I have conducted this activity with thousands of teachers over the years and will share some commonalities in their lists. I'll bet that you'll see more than a few similarities with your own list.

- ◆ My favorite teacher was nice.
- ◆ My favorite teacher made me feel special.
- ◆ My favorite teacher smiled a lot.
- ◆ My favorite teacher found ways to make me succeed.
- ◆ My favorite teacher made learning fun.
- ◆ My favorite teacher did not yell at me or embarrass me in front of my peers.
- ◆ My favorite teacher treated me with respect.
- ◆ My favorite teacher did not struggle with discipline problems.
- ◆ My favorite teacher inspired me.
- ◆ My favorite teacher made lessons interesting.
- ◆ My favorite teacher loved teaching.
- ◆ My favorite teacher loved children.

Did you find some similarities with your own list? Notice that nothing in that list tells about the teacher's credentials. I have yet to find someone to say, "My favorite teacher had three college degrees." And notice that nothing in that list tells of the amount of material that the teacher had students memorize. And take special notice that the list tends to focus on the teacher as a person and how that teacher made students feel—special, loved, successful, inspired.

Question: Would your students list similar characteristics about you?

By the nature of your position, you will influence the life of every student you teach. Whether that influence is a positive or negative one, it will most certainly be a lasting one!

Remember Your "Least Favorite" Teacher

In the previous tip, I had you list the characteristics of your favorite teacher. This time, we will repeat the same process, except that you will be listing the characteristics of your least favorite teacher. Remember not to read on until you have called up the image of this person and listed several characteristics.

Just as in the previous tip, I have conducted this activity with thousands of teachers and have found uncanny similarities in their lists. You will likely see more than a few similarities with your own list.

- ◆ My least favorite teacher was not a very nice person.
- ◆ My least favorite teacher rarely smiled.
- ◆ My least favorite teacher didn't care if I succeeded.
- ◆ My least favorite teacher's class was boring.
- ◆ My least favorite teacher yelled at students and humiliated them.
- ◆ My least favorite teacher treated students disrespectfully.
- ◆ My least favorite teacher had lots of discipline problems.
- ◆ My least favorite teacher did not inspire me.
- ◆ My least favorite teacher did not like teaching.
- ◆ My least favorite teacher did not like children.

Note that the above characteristics are in direct opposition to the characteristics in the previous tip. Also note that your feelings about your least favorite teacher are the antithesis of your feelings about your favorite teacher. I have often seen adults conjure up sadness and anger when remembering their least favorite teacher. Most can remember, in the minutest of detail, specific things that this teacher said or did to hurt or upset them. Usually, these incidents occurred years ago, yet just thinking about their least favorite teacher brings those unpleasant feelings back to the surface. Also, I have yet to find anyone who says the following: "My least favorite teacher really inspired me, but I just didn't like him." The fact is that if you can convince a student that you care, if you can inspire him, and if you can help him succeed, you will always fall into the favorite teacher category. So remember your least favorite and favorite teachers, and use their lessons to remind you of what you do and do NOT want to represent in your students' lives.

Remember, your influence will long outlive you. Leave a positive legacy!

If you plan for a year, plant a seed.
If for ten years, plant a tree.
If for a hundred years, teach the people.
When you sow a seed once, you will reap a
single harvest.
When you teach the people, you will reap a
hundred harvests.

Kuan Chung

Inspire for a Lifetime

Students are much more in need of inspiration than they are of information. The information we provide is important, but the inspiration we provide is life-altering. An inspired individual will achieve great things. An informed individual will accomplish nothing if he lacks inspiration.

It has been said that when a butterfly just moves its wings off the California coast, it flutters the breezes that rustle the leaves on the islands of Japan. The connection is that subtle. Our influence as teachers is lifelong, and it is important that we recognize and capitalize on that fact. If you inspire one student, you affect his entire future, and you literally change the world. Through your actions as a teacher, you have the opportunity to inspire every student who ever walks through your classroom doors. You, as a teacher, are changing this world, one student at a time. What an awesome responsibility! May you never take it lightly.

Great teachers inspire and set their students' minds afire!

Keep an "I Am Special" Folder

Whether you are a new or veteran teacher, it's never too late to start keeping an "I Am Special" folder. It's a very simple concept with very special rewards. An "I Am Special" folder is a folder in which you will keep notes from students, thank-you cards, letters of appreciation, notes to yourself on something exciting or heartwarming that happens to you on a particular day, letters from parents, etc. And on those really difficult days when you are questioning whether you truly are making a difference, just take out the folder and begin to look through it. It will reaffirm the fact that you are making a difference, it will rekindle your love of children and teaching, and it will remind you that you have truly chosen the noblest of all professions—teaching!

A high school coach recently reminded me that I had given him an "I Am Special" folder when he had come through one of my new-teacher trainings a few years prior. He shared with me that he thought the idea of keeping such a folder was probably more appropriate for elementary teachers, but he decided to give it a try regardless. He told me that he began keeping newspaper clippings from games, notes from players, notes from parents, and notes he had written on occasion when he felt he had been able to light a spark in one of his players. He proudly told me that his folder had gotten so thick that he had to start a second one!

As teachers, we are special to so many students. But sometimes we need a reminder. An "I Am Special" folder will do the trick! I still have mine, and it is one of my most valued possessions.

Tip 99

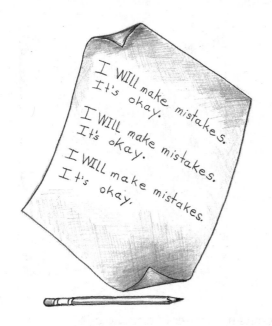

The Biggest Mistake

*The biggest mistake that you can make is to
be afraid of making a mistake
For if you're afraid to make a mistake, no
risks or chances will you take
And if no risks or chances you take, and if
you put nothing of yourself at stake
You'll walk through life asleep, not awake,
and not one difference will you make!*

A.L.B.

Teach Students that Mistakes Are Wonderful Leaning Opportunities

What happened to you the first time you tried to ride a bicycle on your own? You fell. The first time you tried to tie your own shoelaces? It didn't *quite* work out. What is typically the first word that a baby speaks? Da-da. I've checked the dictionary, and there's no such word. The baby makes a *mistake*. And what do we do, as parents? We praise the mistake and encourage the baby. We call everyone we know to tell them that our baby has spoken his first word. We even go so far as to start making the mistake ourselves, saying, "Where's da-da?" We would never dream of saying, "No, don't say that," to the baby. And we definitely would never think of labeling him a *non-talker*. This is because parents know that this *mistake* is a necessary part of learning to speak. All parents know that the *mistake* will eventually correct itself, so not only do they not worry about it, but they encourage the child's many mistakes as he learns to speak. Oh, and the good news is that I have yet to meet an adult who still calls his father "da-da."

Isn't it true that we learn best through our mistakes? Skinned knees are a part of learning to ride a bike. Burnt meals are a part of learning to cook. Think back to your first year of teaching. If you're a first-year teacher, think back to yesterday. Didn't you make mistakes? No matter how long you've been teaching, you will still make mistakes. So why is it that, in many classrooms, mistakes are viewed as unacceptable? Why is it that we don't hear enough teachers saying, "Great! You made a mistake. Now let's see what we can learn from it." I am not suggesting that we never point out students' mistakes. I am suggesting that we make it *okay* to make mistakes in our classrooms. We should encourage students to take risks, make mistakes, and then learn from them. The greatest mistake any student can make is to stop trying for fear of failing. And the greatest mistake any teacher can make is to encourage that type of behavior.

The very best teachers are continually making their classrooms havens for student risk-taking!

I promise never to give up on you,
no matter what you say or do
For I am your teacher and teach you I will
Even if you give up, I'll believe in you still.

Refuse to Give Up on Any Child

It is when we think we have exhausted all resources that we should resolve never to stop trying. It is when a child tries our patience to the very end that we must muster even more patience. It is when we think we can't that we should. It should be with utmost resolve that we refuse to give up on any student. It should be with resolute determination that we commit to making every child successful, no matter what it takes. And when a child is not experiencing success, we, as teachers, must change our approach—and keep changing that approach until we find one that works.

Remember the following:

- ♦ Every child is someone special.
- ♦ Every child deserves a fair chance.
- ♦ Every child deserves a capable, caring, competent teacher.
- ♦ Every child deserves to be treated with dignity and respect.
- ♦ Every child is capable of success.
- ♦ Every child has strengths that need to be recognized and nurtured.
- ♦ Every child truly wants to succeed.
- ♦ Every child craves love and appreciation, which every teacher should provide.

Find the beauty in each child that often lies hidden behind life's layers of protection. Find it. It is your responsibility. It is your privilege. It is your calling. Work your magic!

Tip 101

Plus 7 More!

*Just in case 101 is not enough,
here are seven more—more really good stuff!*

*If you deal with even the toughest
of students privately, one on one,
Then chances increase that instead
of striking out, you just might
score a homerun!*

Hold Private Practice Sessions

FACT: If you deal with a student's misbehavior in front of the class, the behavior will rarely improve. It may even worsen, because the student will have an *audience*. But when you deal with students privately, even the toughest of students are suddenly not so tough. The following strategy is practically magic. You will be amazed at its positive results.

Let's say that a student is a chronic talker. Simply talk to the student privately and say, "I noticed that you're having trouble remembering our procedure for raising your hand before speaking. Don't be too hard on yourself for forgetting. I forget things, too. But I know how embarrassing it can be to forget so often in front of your friends, so I'll do a favor for you. I'll give you my recess today and I'll practice that procedure with you so that you'll get better at it and won't forget so much. I'm happy to do that for you. See you at recess." That's it. What you're doing is pretending to think that the student is simply forgetting to raise his hand. Surely he would not be ignoring the procedure purposefully! The key is that you are not at all sarcastic and that you tell him that you are giving of your own time to help him. So instead of taking his recess from him, you're giving him yours!

So the student comes in at recess and you say, "Thanks for coming in. Now pretend that you are in class and you have something to say. Show me what you will do." The students slowly raises his hand, and you say, "Great! I can give you fifteen more minutes of practice. Do you need more practice or do you think you have it?" The student always says, "I have it." Then say, "Great. See you tomorrow. Oh, and if you forget again, that's my fault. It simply means I didn't give you enough practice time. I'll even stay after school if you need. Just let me know."

Please note that the technique takes less than a minute, so you will not lose your recess. And if you teach in a school where there is no recess, you can use this quick technique between classes, during your planning period, during lunchtime, etc.

You'll be amazed at the results if you use this technique appropriately. But if your approach even hints at sarcasm, it will not work.

When the student next returns to your class, be sure to catch him when he is *not* talking and thank him. If the problem ever becomes chronic again, simply have another private practice session. You can use this for practically any sort of misbehavior.

The *private practice session* strategy is a simple one that produces amazing results. It is used successfully at all grade levels. Anyone who tells you that this technique does not work has obviously never tried it. Practice makes perfect, doesn't it? So practice, practice, practice, and watch behavior improve, improve, improve.

Tip from Breaux, A. & Whitaker, T. (2010). *50 Ways to Improve Student Behavior.* Larchmont, NY: Eye On Education.

If you want your students to pass,
Test what you teach them in class.
Don't let what they learn on their
own prevail
As what decides whether they pass
or fail.

Take Responsibility for Whether Your Students Pass or Fail

A teacher was speaking to me about one of her students. The conversation went like this:

> *"It's a shame that he is failing my class, because he is so capable."*
> *"Why is he failing?" I asked.*
> *"Because he refuses to study, and he admits it. His mother even admits that he doesn't study."*
> *I then asked, "Oh, so you only test your students on what they learn at home?"*
> *Confused, she asked, "What do you mean?"*
> *"Well," I asked, "is he not participating in class?"*
> *"That's the problem," she said. "He participates in class and he really doesn't cause any problems, but he doesn't study his notes."*
> *I explained to her that she was basically admitting that she was not actually testing skills but rather having students go home and memorize notes to spit back on a test. I finally got her to realize that a test is supposed to be a measure of skills learned in class as opposed to facts memorized at home. I then asked, "When your principal evaluates you, does he evaluate you on your teaching skills that you demonstrate in class or does he have you go home and memorize notes on the history of teaching and then grade you based solely on your written test results?"*
> *"Oh my goodness!" she exclaimed, "Now I realize what you are saying."*

Long story short, she changed her entire approach to teaching and testing. She thanks me to this day for that conversation which provided the inspiration for this poem:

Whether My Students Pass or Fail

He did not pass my test because he didn't study
And so I took my red pen and made his paper bloody
And then I started thinking about what I was doing
What in the world was I trying to prove—what point was I pursuing?
If studying determined his grade, what had I really taught?
If studying was the only way to pass, in class no learning was wrought
Yes, studying is important, but teaching should mean more
If I'm really teaching every day, it should affect his score
Studying might mean the difference between an A and a B
But whether my students pass or fail really depends on ME!

A.L.B.

If you've lost control or let things slide, don't
run, don't cry, don't try to hide,
Don't fret, don't fuss, don't give up or give in
Just treat it as day one—ready, set, begin!

Start Over on ANY Day!

A new teacher said to me, "I've lost control of the students. But it's the middle of the school year. Isn't it too late to start over?" My answer to her and my answer to you is that, though it is easier if you have established and maintained control from the first day of school than it is to *regain* control once it has been lost, it is never too late to start over. So all is not lost, even though it may seem that way to a person who has lost control.

The following is a little *trick* for starting over on any day. Whenever you want to try something new, due to the fact that what you were doing was not working, use the *teacher meeting* trick. It goes like this:

> *Let's say that students are talking out of turn a lot, and the behavior is getting worse. Instead of saying, "You've gotten out of control with your talking, so I'm going to start punishing you from today on if you talk out of turn," simply say, "I attended a teacher meeting and we were discussing sixth-grade procedures. I know you're only fifth graders, but I told the teachers at the meeting that my fifth graders could handle this procedure. Would you like to try it?" They always agree, and you set your new procedure for talking. You practice it and make them successful and praise them, and then you practice and make them successful and praise them, over and over. Then you say, "Wow, I can't wait to tell everyone at the next teacher meeting that you all are able to handle sixth-grade procedures! I'm so proud of you."*

Now you've just established a new procedure and you have made it fun and attainable. Just follow through and be consistent and continue to set them up for success. If one student is not following the procedure, use the *private practice session* we discussed in Tip 102. You can use the *teacher meeting* trick for any grade level, by the way. You can use it to regain control, or you can use it to establish any new procedures you may wish to establish. Who cares if your students think you attend weekly teacher meetings?

Don't waste time fretting over past mistakes or failed attempts at establishing and maintaining control. Rather, analyze what did not work, learn from it, and start over! Usually, when teachers lose control of management or when procedures do not work, it reflects a lack of consistency on the part of the teacher. **So establish your procedures, be consistent in implementing them, never lose control of yourself, and chances are good that you will not lose control of your students.**

There's something called a teacher's desk, and
its purpose is for storage
It holds all your stuff so that when you need
something, you know just where to forage.

Get Out from Behind the Desk!

There is a piece of furniture in every classroom known as the teacher's desk. If you are a new teacher, have you figured out the purpose of that piece of furniture? If not, I'll tell you. There are actually two purposes: 1) to store stuff, and 2) to sit at when students are not in the room. Period! There are no other purposes for that piece of furniture. BUT, many teachers have never received that memo, and they actually sit at their desks while the students are in the room! Some practically LIVE there! That's a huge mistake. Here's why: A physical barrier equals a mental barrier! It physically separates people, thus emotionally separating them. And the LAST thing you want is to be emotionally separated from your students. You want them to know that you are just like a coach, right in the game with them. (Please notice that there is never a coach's desk on the sideline of a football field.) Feel free to sit at your desk in order to do paperwork any time that the students are not present. But when the students are present, even when they are working independently, it is vital that you are *in the game* with them. As we have already discussed (see Tip 13), the closer you are in proximity to your students, the less likely they are to misbehave and the more likely they are to remain engaged in their studies. So get out from behind that desk! If, for some reason, you must occasionally sit while teaching, simply take your chair from behind your desk and put it right in the center of your students. This way, you are still with them, as opposed to physically separating yourself from them.

You're not a judge in a courtroom, on a raised platform behind the "bench"
But rather you're a teacher of thirsty students whose thirst is yours to quench!
Students should not need permission to approach
Or be warned that on your space they must not encroach
For you're not a judge in a courtroom, you're a teacher, the ultimate coach
The person who, more than any other, is completely safe to approach!

Tip 105

YOUR reaction is the main attraction. It can ignite or extinguish a behavior infraction.

Defuse Disrespectful Students

It was the first day of school and in walked Albert Wilson. He was almost 16 years old and in the seventh grade, and he was determined to make certain his teacher, Ms. Adams, knew to leave him alone. He would soon be quitting school and had no intentions of doing any work. Albert was in for a big surprise, however. What he didn't know was that Ms. Adams understood the psychology of dealing with disrespectful students. As Ms. Adams was walking around assisting students with their work, she noticed Albert staring at her, waiting for her to get closer. As she approached his desk, he held his pencil up next to her and angrily snapped it in two, as if to say, "I'll show you!" Ms. Adams, needing time to think of how best to handle this, walked slowly to her can of used pencils, found a short one with no eraser left on it, walked back to Albert's desk, and handed it to him. She said, "Albert, I understand your frustration. But in the future, if you feel you need to break a pencil, just let me know and I'll give you one of my old ones."

Do you see what she did? She completely defused him by not allowing him to *get the best of her.* She continued to treat Albert kindly and calmly. She chose to place his future success in her class ahead of her own need to "win" the battle. Had she not displayed restraint, she may have allowed her emotions to rule her reactions, thereby ensuring that Albert would remain a victim of himself and she a victim of Albert. Less effective teachers would have probably gotten into a battle of words, ordered him out of the room, or sent him to the office.

Albert, by the way, did not quit school. In fact, he finished the year and moved on to the next grade. He came to trust Mrs. Adams with academic and personal issues during the time he spent in her classroom. And though he may have broken several pencil points while working diligently, he never broke a pencil in anger again!

Remember that you always have a choice. You can choose to engage in a power struggle with a student or you can choose to defuse the misbehavior. CHOOSE to DEFUSE!

Tip from Breaux, A. & Breaux, E. (2004). *REAL Teachers, REAL Challenges, REAL Solutions.* Larchmont, NY: Eye On Education.

Tip 106

The louder you speak, the less others take heed;
a soft, calm voice is what students need!

Speak Awfully Softly

Have you ever noticed that great teachers' voices are soothingly calm and pleasant? This is because they know that when they speak softly, students seem to feel that what these teachers have to say is important. The opposite seems to prevail in less-than-effective teachers' classrooms. **A soft voice tends to express caring and concern. A loud voice tends to express aggravation and agitation.** Teachers' voices are best and most influential when calm and soothing, yet loud enough, of course, for the students to hear. Consider the following scenario:

> *A student is upset and expressing anger toward another classmate. The confrontation is escalating, and the student's anger is building. His voice is getting louder. Enter the loud teacher... The teacher begins to scream at the student, telling him to stop it and to calm down. But nothing about the teacher's actions is conducive to ending a confrontation. Nothing about the teacher is calm. The teacher is actually fueling the flame. This never works. Rather, a calm, professional approach is the only way to calm an angry student. The louder the student gets, the softer you, the teacher, must become. By the way, this works with adults, too! Fires require fuel to burn. Don't feed the fire!*

When faced with a confrontational student, an effective teacher remains calm. His voice remains soothing, yet serious. He speaks with the student as opposed to screaming at him. Oftentimes, he tells the student that he will give him a few minutes to cool down, and then he will speak to the student.

The bottom line is that a soft voice portrays a calm demeanor. A calm demeanor is contagious, thus leading to a calmer environment. Calm environments are conducive to good student behavior. So speak awfully softly!

Tip from Breaux, A. & Whitaker, T. (2010). *50 Ways to Improve Student Behavior*. Larchmont, NY: Eye On Education.

Tip 107

Wear the Title "Teacher" Proudly

*"Oh take off your rosy glasses," says a
    teacher as she passes,*
*For she sees my new excitement almost like
    it's her indictment*
*Of her dreadful misery, my-oh-my-oh-my-
    oh me!*
*But another teacher passes who still wears
    rose-colored glasses.*
*She has worn them 30 years, for she loves
    the little dears*
*That she teaches every day,
    yea-oh-yea-oh-yea-oh-yea!*
So my excitement's not for naught; I can love all days I've taught
And I know the choice is mine; I can cheer or I can whine
And at the end of 30 years, I hope that you can hear me loudly
As I still recite my cheers and wear the title "Teacher" proudly!

A.L.B.

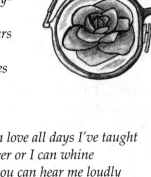

Keep Your Rose-Colored Glasses On

If, at any stage in your career, you lose your rose-colored glasses, it is probably time to find a new career. On any faculty (remember Mrs. WarnYa from Tip 49), there are teachers who have long ago lost their rose-colored glasses and have simply *forgotten* to quit or retire. They are quick to find the new teachers and share their lack of enthusiasm for teaching, students, and the profession. Don't participate. Here's a simple trick for defusing those who have lost their love of teaching:

> *Let's say that a non-rose-colored-glasses-wearing teacher approaches you and begins to warn you about certain trouble-causing students. Simply say, "Thanks so much for telling me about them. Those are the kinds of students who need me the most, so I'll give them extra special attention. You must care a lot about them to have shared their stories with me. Again, thanks so much." And walk away with a smile on your face. It works every time!*

And here's one more trick:

> *Let's say that one of these same teachers approaches you with some type of gossip about a student, a coworker, etc. Simply say, "I'd love to talk to you, but I'm in a rush to get to the restroom before the bell rings." That, too, works like a charm because they simply find another target on which to unload their gossip.*

Remember, don't participate in anything that requires that you remove your rose-colored glasses. You can remain a positive, caring, hard-working, influential, effective teacher all the days of your career.

Students LOVE the classes of teachers with rose-colored glasses!

Tip 108

Conclusion

I hope that this book has served to provide you with answers, with questions, and with inspiration. Thank you for making a difference. Thank you for touching young lives. Thank you for changing this world, one child at a time. Thank you for daring to teach!

If You So Dare

If you so endeavor to seek and to find
How to light a spark in one child's mind
Then you have endeavored to change the world
Far beyond just that one boy or girl
For once one spark is lit, you see
It ignites a fire that spreads easily
And so by touching just one child
You took one step that spanned a mile
For you never know just how far-reaching
Will be your influence while you are teaching
So teach each one with caution and care
And change the world, if you so dare!

A.L.B.

We also recommend…

REAL Teachers, REAL Challenges, REAL Solutions:

25 Ways to Handle the Challenges of the Classroom Effectively

Annette and Elizabeth Breaux

"After reading this book, your teaching will never be the same. It is a must read for all teachers."

Harry K. Wong, Author of
The First Days of School

For new teacher induction programs or high-interest staff development workshops, this book helps new teachers—and experienced ones—find solutions to common classroom challenges. It shows teachers how to get students to do what you want them to do, deal with parents and difficult co-workers, and solve other common teaching challenges.

It presents 25 real scenarios along with "What's Effective," "What's NOT Effective," and "Bottom Line" strategies for handling teacher challenges.

2004, 120 pp. paperback 1-930556-64-0

Seven Simple Secrets:
What the BEST Teachers Know and Do!
Annette Breaux and Todd Whitaker

"A wonderful book for new teachers and their mentors."

Sharon Weber, Principal
Bell Township Elementary School, PA

This book reveals—
- The Secret of Classroom Management
- The Secret of Instruction
- The Secret of Attitude
- The Secret of Professionalism
- The Secret of Effective Discipline
- The Secret of Motivation and Inspiration

Implementing these secrets will change your life, both in and out of the classroom. But most importantly, implementing these secrets will enhance the lives of every student you teach.

2006, 160 pp. paperback 1-59667-021-5

10 Days to Maximum Teaching Success
Annette L. Breaux

10 Days to Maximum Teaching Success is an exciting, innovative approach to staff development, mentoring, and new teacher induction...on AUDIO CDs! Ten highly interactive audio sessions on four CDs that train teachers to maximize their effectiveness. Your teachers implement daily assignments, work through over 50 activities, and track daily progress in their Personal Achievement Logs (PAL). With a special BONUS SESSION: Achieving Financial Independence on a Teacher's Salary. Each session lasts about 20 minutes. Teachers track their progress and complete interactive assignments in their Personal Achievement Log (PAL). The PAL is not just a journal. It also includes a wealth of information regarding each session along with specific instructions for teachers to follow as they implement what they have learned in their classrooms.

Covered in 10 Days to Maximum Teaching Success are the following topics:
♦ Classroom Management
♦ Discipline
♦ Effective Teaching Strategies
♦ Planning
♦ Controlling Your Actions and Reactions w/Students
♦ Professionalism

2005, CD-Audio 978-1-93055-690-4

50 Ways to Improve Student Behavior:
Simple Solutions to Complex Challenges
Annette L. Breaux and Todd Whitaker

From best-selling authors Annette Breaux and Todd Whitaker, *50 Ways to Improve Student Behavior: Simple Solutions to Complex Challenges* is a must-read reference for teachers, both new and experienced!

In a lively and engaging style, Annette Breaux and Todd Whitaker share 50 simple, straightforward techniques for improving student behavior and increasing student cooperation, participation, and achievement. Each practical, well-defined strategy can be applied in classrooms of all grade levels and subjects. Strategies include:

- How to make students more responsible
- How to nip potential problems in the bud
- Learning what to overlook
- Establishing classroom rules and procedures
- Teaching in small bites (It makes students hungrier!)

As student behavior improves, so too will the quality of learning in your classroom. With this book, you can begin to introduce a host of new strategies into your teaching practice today!

2010, 144 pp. paperback 978-1-59667-132-4

101 Poems for Teachers
Annette L. Breaux

One of the most sought-after and dynamic speakers in education, Annette Breaux has inspired audiences of teachers and administrators across the country. She has incorporated each of her presentations with her heartwarming original poetry. This collection brings together 101 of Breaux's poems, from which teachers and school staff can draw continued motivation and enjoyment.

I Teach

I light a spark in a darkened soul
I warm the heart of one grown cold
I look beyond and see within
Behind the face, beneath the skin
I quench a thirst, I soothe a pain
I provide the food that will sustain
I touch, I love, I laugh, I cry
Whatever is needed, I supply
Yet more than I give, I gain from each
I am most richly blessed—I teach!

—*Annette Breaux*

2010, 208 pp. paperback 978-1-59667-146-1

Notes